PREACHING ON
SPECIAL OCCASIONS

D. W. Cleverley Ford

MOWBRAYS

LONDON & OXFORD

First published 1975
by A. R. Mowbray & Co. Ltd,
The Alden Press, Osney Mead,
Oxford OX2 0EG

ISBN 0 264 66101 X

Text set in 12 pt Monotype Bembo, printed by letterpress, and bound in Great Britain
at The Pitman Press, Bath

PREFACE

This book has been written at the invitation of Richard Mulkern of the Publishing Division of Messrs A. R. Mowbray, to whom I am also indebted for many helpful suggestions concerning its presentation. I must also express my thanks once again to Mrs J. Hodgson for typing and re-typing my manuscript and for checking the proofs.

Lambeth 1975   *D. W. Cleverley Ford*

CONTENTS

INTRODUCTION

During the year 1942, in London, a woman in Red Cross uniform looked back across the years that separated her from herself as the girl who arrived from the United States in 1913 with her father for a fortnight's holiday in England. Rain fell almost incessantly throughout the period. They lodged in an unprepossessing boarding house in Bloomsbury and saw little of London. But one special occasion did occur on the eve of their departure. The girl was invited to a Ball in Park Lane. Her unexpected host was an elderly man in the boarding house who would not have used his invitation had no partner appeared to accompany him. But there was this girl. So they dressed and attended the Ball. It was indeed a special occasion. The Ball Room itself, the distinguished company, the uniforms, the dresses and the music were sufficient in themselves to make it so. But even the special occasion took on special significance. The American girl met the man she was to marry, an Englishman, so the meeting changed her life. And how it had changed! Her husband came to be killed shortly before the armistice in 1918 and now her son was involved in the Navy in the Dieppe Raid of 1942. As she sat tensely waiting for news, her mind raced back over the years to that special occasion in 1913. Everything in her life had changed because that special occasion took on special significance.

Once or twice in all our lives, perhaps more than once or twice, we find ourselves attending some special occasion. Not perhaps so grand as a Ball in Park Lane, but a child's baptism or a service for nurses, a Retreat or even some Church Festival. On occasions such as these, it is often the privilege, but also the terror for a priest or minister to be invited to give an address. Even without the address these occasions would have sufficient in themselves to make them special. A whole family present. An unusually large gathering of the members of some profession. A few days quiet in a house set apart for Retreats. The expectancy of a major Church Festival. The preacher's responsibility, however, is to try and make the special occasion take on special significance, so much so that some person present may perhaps confess after the passage of years, 'How my life has changed! And how much is due to that special occasion which I can never forget. Something happened for me which altered my perspectives.'

Is this a possibility as a direct result of a sermon on a special occasion? The question in itself is almost sufficient to frighten away all but the most insensitive from accepting such an invitation. For the sermon on the special occasion to fall flat, ring untrue or simply sound banal, is all too easy, doubling the disappointment. There will be few preachers unwilling, therefore, to accept some help, and surely none at all so sure of themselves, not to seek the empowering of the Divine Spirit, who alone can make these special occasions take on special significance.

CHRISTMAS

The visible word

Jeremiah 1. 11 (RSV) *And the word of the Lord came to me, saying, "What do you see?" '*

In the Old Testament there is a phrase which is used over and over again, so frequently, perhaps, that we fail to notice how strange it is; it is the phrase, 'And the word of the Lord came to me saying . . . .' It could be, however, that you yourself have used a similar phrase. You might have remarked, 'I had puzzled and puzzled over that problem when all of a sudden the answer came to me.' Or you might meet a writer who will confess, 'Somehow that book seemed to write itself. It raised no problems. The whole thing came to me out of the blue.' Perhaps George Frederic Handel said something like this in 1742 when the *Messiah* was first performed in Dublin and was at once acclaimed, never ceasing to be the most popular piece of music, especially at Christmas. 'The music just came to me.'

1 *The word of the Lord comes to us*

But does anything exist 'outside' that is able to come to us? Must we not assert that what appears to come to us from outside is really only an uprush from our subconscious mind? Handel's *Messiah*, for example, is composed of all sorts of arias and refrains from various sources that had sunk down into Handel's subconscious personality as he heard them, even unknowingly, but one day they burst forth as a new creation. A great many people would take this view.

Christmas, however, says the opposite. It declares that there is something distinct and apart from men, something they have not invented, nor even discovered, but which comes to people. This is the meaning of the Incarnation, the meaning of the Virgin Birth, the meaning of the baby in the manger.

> '*He came down to earth from heaven*
> *Who is God and Lord of all,*
> *And his shelter was a stable,*
> *And his cradle was a stall;*'
> (Mrs C. F. Alexander)

We don't, of course, imply that heaven is above the sky or that it is spatially remote from us 'out there'. What Christmas proclaims is that men, this world and our problems are not the only realities, there is also God. Properly understood, Christmas is not merely a time of cosy good will, sentimental and wishful thinking for peace; first and foremost Christmas is a powerful rebuttal of atheism. It calls aloud that God exists.

And not only that God exists, but that God comes to us, takes the initiative and breaks in on our routine. In the year 1918 a new and strident prophetic voice was heard in Switzerland since when no Christian thinking has ever been quite the same the world over, however much that theology came to be criticised and adjusted. This was Karl Barth. For German philosophical rationalism had turned God into an object of intellectual pursuit until God was irrelevant over against the supposed ingenuity of men. God had become an idea, a hypothesis, almost a thing. Karl Barth, however, a man of great intellectual stature, (metaphorically speaking) took the high and dry intellectualised Christian public by the scruff of its neck and shouted 'No, all our clever philosophies get us nowhere. They can never reach the real God. They can never save us from calamity. They are like a broken bridge which can never span the chasm between man and God. They can only be bridged by God moving out to us from his side.' And this is what Christmas means.

> 'He came down to earth from heaven
> Who is God and Lord of all,
> And his shelter was a stable,
> And his cradle was a stall;'

There is a phrase in the Bible for this action and initiative of God. It is 'the word of the Lord.' It occurs over and over again in the Old Testament. It is embodied in my text for this Christmas Day. 'And the word of the Lord came to me, saying . . . .' And the most significant of all the occurrences is in the New Testament in the Gospel for today. 'And the Word became flesh and dwelt among us.' The strong message of Christmas is that God not only exists, he comes to us. This is the word of the Lord.

2 The visible word

We return to the text from Jeremiah. 'And the word of the Lord came to me, saying . . . .' and we expect something which has to

4

be listened to. Nine times out of ten indeed this is the case in the Old Testament, but not here in my text, 'And the word of the Lord came to me, saying, "What do you *see*?" ' Here in the first chapter of Jeremiah, what Jeremiah was made to see was an almond tree in full blossom, the kind of sight that will begin to gladden our eyes in about ten weeks' time as an harbinger of spring. And Jeremiah was made to look again and he saw 'a cauldron on a fire fanned by the wind.' Both the almond tree that day and the seething cauldron that day, where he saw them, became for him the word of the Lord. They spoke to him.

And this is frequently how God works. This is how it was at Bethlehem. God did not shout from heaven, 'I am God alone and I came for all men everywhere.' Instead he came as a baby in a manger, a cattle shed for a maternity home, shepherds straight from the fields for a mother's first visitors, and no medical attention of any kind. 'And the word of the Lord came to me, saying, "What do you see?" '

And the same question is addressed to us this Christmas Day. What do you see? A pretty picture only, fit decoration for a Christmas card? Or something tremendous, namely that God shows by his actions that he not only exists but that he cares sufficiently about mankind to come to be among us.

> '*He came down to earth from heaven*
> *Who is God and Lord of all,*
> *And his shelter was a stable,*
> *And his cradle was a stall;*
> *With the poor and mean and lowly*
> *Lived on earth our Saviour holy.*'

'And the word of the Lord came unto me, saying, "What do you see?" ' That action of God at Bethlehem is not only historical, it is existential. It does not only take place in Judaea, it takes place now in this locality. Here is a man refusing to take an increase in wages so that some one else less well-paid than he may have a rise. Here is a woman agreeing to work throughout the Christmas holidays so that another employee may have the break she more desperately needs.

'And the word of the Lord came to me, saying, "What do you see?" '

Two crazy idealists? Is that all you see? Or is this the Spirit of God acting in humble and most unexpected people?

*'He came down to earth from heaven
Who is God and Lord of all,
And his shelter was a stable,
And his cradle was a stall;'*

Look around you, my friends. God is not shouting his message from heaven. He rarely does, but he comes to us from heaven to act in the lives of the most unexpected people and the most unexpected places. Keep your eyes open and when you see evidence of God at work, believe what you see, and go on your way rejoicing. 'Emmanuel. God is with us.'

3 *Confidence*

A short time ago two small boys woke up, noticed that the sun was already shining and called for their mother. But no reply came. They called again loudly this time and more insistently, but still no answer. Then greatly wondering, they tip-toed along to the kitchen, but she wasn't there. Nor was she in her bedroom. To their horror they discovered that the flat was empty, so they hurried out on to the landing of the block of flats searching everywhere, too terrified to cry. Finally, they crept back to their own beds and to what seemed an eternity. Last of all, however, they heard her steps in the passage and ran to greet her. She had only been delayed in a traffic jam in an early morning dash to the supermarket. But what a difference her presence made! All the fear of an empty flat disappeared in an instant to be replaced by laughter and joy.

Here is the unspoken question that lies heavily on ten thousand hearts today. Is ours an empty world? Has God left us? Has he forgotten us? Is there indeed a God at all to care what becomes of us? But at Christmas we hear his steps in the passage and what could be described as 'the word of the Lord coming to us and saying, "What do you see?" ' And we look, and there is the baby in the manger, 'who is God and Lord of all.' So we know everything will be all right and we can go on our way with a light heart for God is with us still and he cares . . .

Drawing the poison

Psalm 14. 4–5 *'But they are all gone out of the way, they are altogether become abominable: there is none that doeth good, no not one. Their throat is an open sepulchre, with their tongues have they deceived: the poison of asps is under their lips.'*

I begin with an activity so commonplace, so ordinary I am almost ashamed to employ it, but it contains, I think, the possibility of an analogy capable of helping us as we begin our meditation on the Cross of Jesus Christ. It concerns a man pruning roses in his garden and when he has finished, becoming aware of a stabbing pain in one of his fingers, but he pays little attention. Next day, however, the pain intensifies and by the third day his finger is badly swollen. He seeks advice, as a result of which a seriously poisoned finger is diagnosed, which, unless it receives the appropriate attention, could result in amputation. And the remedy comprises medical dressings, which perform the function of an old-fashioned poultice, drawing the poison to the surface, so that it can be drained away and the finger set on the path to healing. But the operation is painful, indeed, for a time the cure is worse than the cause; the poison must, however, be drawn, otherwise no healthy finger will result.

I suggest that the crucifixion of Christ taking place within the community operates as does a poultice. It draws the poison to the surface and our first task could well be to see how this was so historically.

1 *The Cross in history*

The crucifixion of Jesus began with plots behind closed doors, organized so early in the ministry that they could properly be recorded in only the second chapter of St Mark's gospel. We read that after the healing by Jesus of the paralysed man let down through a roof by four friends, and after the call of Levi to be an apostle, and the conflict with the Pharisees because the disciples plucked ears of corn on the Sabbath, yes, as early as this in the ministry, the Pharisees and the Herodians (an ungodly alliance if ever there was one), plotted to liquidate him. And these men, joined subsequently by the legal experts and the religious leaders never wearied of harassing him, posing awkward questions, laying subtle traps and confronting him with embarrassing situations,

7

everything aimed at engineering him into a corner where they might discredit him, and in the end condemn him. But their crafty tactics miscarried, or would have miscarried, had not Judas, one of his followers, betrayed his master; whereupon all the venom flowing through their veins gathered into one nefarious act of scandalous hostility, they crucified him. And with it went the sudden arrest at night, the hurried trial and trumped-up charges, the humiliation of the victim, the torture; and around the fringe of all this cruelty was bribery, and working upon the feelings of the crowd and the chanting of slogans, all the tactics to which we have become sickeningly accustomed in our age of violence. And the end product? A quasi-theatrical exhibition of one unfortunate man stripped of his clothes and self-respect, nailed to a piece of wood to die in public, slowly, agonizingly and utterly alone, a throw-out from respectable society, broken between the wheels of Jewish intrigue and Roman imperial power. And on this festering sore at Calvary there settled all the flies of blood-lust, cruelty and graft, so that I am bound to say that the first visible effect of the crucifixion of Jesus was to draw to the surface the poison that lies hidden below the surface of society, mostly unsuspected.

In a school in South London some months ago a disturbing case of child-bullying was brought to the public notice by means of the press. A teen-age girl was rendered so wretched by the treatment meted out to her by her schoolmates that she took her own life. The mind boggles at the misery to which this girl must have been reduced to have recourse to such desperate remedy as suicide. And the mind boggles at boys and girls finding it in themselves so to victimise one of their number that she came to hate life itself. And not the least part of the tragedy is that there seems to have been no one in whom she could confide, she was utterly alone.

We find it hard to believe that poison does exist below the apparently civilised calm of the community as we know it, but every now and again an incident occurs which opens up a trap door on to what we would prefer to ignore but which Freud relentlessly informed us is actually there, the raw materials of brutal behaviour, covered only at the best of times by a thin crust of partial civilisation.

In the Old Testament in the book of the prophet Isaiah, there are inserted four poems commonly called the *Servant Songs*. They tell of a man gentle in voice and gentle in demeanour—'He shall

8

not cry nor lift up, nor cause his voice to be heard in the street. A bruised reed shall he not break, and the smoking flax shall he not extinguish'; being victimised, 'I gave my back to the smiters and my cheek to them that plucked off the hair. I hid not my face from shame and spitting'; victimised not only in life but even in death, 'they made his grave with the wicked and with the rich in his death although he had done no violence, neither was there deceit in his mouth.'

All this frightening recurring phenomenon of venom in mankind, gathered together into a head by the appearance of one good man in the community, has been realised a thousand times ten thousand. We see the same poison at work when boys and grown men stoop to torture caged animals. And once in the year AD 29 outside Jerusalem's walls this evil urge assumed terrible proportions. When a man appeared in the community so godlike that he could not be refused the title, 'Son of God', 'God Incarnate', 'God in human flesh', men plotted behind closed doors in cold blood to capture him, torment him, crucify him, and spit upon him as he died.

'But they are all gone out of the way, they are altogether become abominable; there is none that doeth good, no not one. Their throat is an open sepulchre, with their tongues have they deceived: the poison of asps is under their lips.'

The first effect of the appearance of Christ among men was to gather all the venom hidden below the surface of society into one ghastly exhibition called the crucifixion of Jesus.

2 *The Cross as a probe*

And now we turn away from the past into the present. We move from the crucifixion of Jesus in AD 29 outside Jerusalem to consider how that cross illuminates our contemporary scene, because it does illuminate it.

Time and time again throughout the ages, discerning men, of whom Isaiah was one, and Jeremiah was another, peered into the heart of man. And there came a day outside Jerusalem's walls when on a hill, selected because it was so macabre as to be shaped like a man's skull, so-called civilized, yes, even so-called religious men caught and crucified their victim, Jesus of Nazareth, and in doing so captured, concentrated and reflected back for all to see the real condition of human nature we would prefer to hide. We see in the heart of apparently healthy man a kind of cancer and the

9

Cross is the X-ray beam which reveals it. And this, be it noted, is the irrefutibility of the diagnosis—the crucifixion of Jesus happened. It is historical. We cannot say that this is not the kind of thing that would take place in a civilised, even religious society, it did take place. Apparently there lies at the heart of man a terrible distortion which makes him even hate the good which he knows to be good.

I ask myself, you must have asked yourself, how can a twenty-year-old in Northern Ireland in the year 1974 hold a complete stranger in his gun sight for two seconds and then press the trigger? How do terrorists find it in their hearts to place a bomb in an aircraft full of innocent passengers? How do we explain the incidence of torture fast becoming a normal police practice in various parts of the world? What is it that Solzhenitsyn is protesting against in Soviet Russia in our times? Is not the reading of history (by a man like A. N. Whitehead) one long terrible story of man's inhumanity to man? The tale of terrible torments in history is factual not imaginary, and who with his eyes open is not alarmed at the increase of violence in our day?

The first effect of the Cross of Christ is to produce a sorry diagnosis of the human condition. 'But they are all gone out of the way, they are altogether become abominable: there is none that doeth good, no not one. Their throat is an open sepulchre, with their tongues have they deceived: the poison of asps is under their lips.'

3 Our protest at the diagnosis

And you want to cry out and I want to cry out, 'No, no, not me! I have never consciously harmed anyone.' No, this I accept, but I would not wish to vouchsafe how I would behave if my background and my circumstances were other than they were and are! I put myself in the shoes of any one of those disciples that fateful week preceding Good Friday, would I have confessed discipleship of Christ knowing that it must lead me to face the execution squad? Nor would I wish to guarantee that I would not resort to some desperate measure in Northern Ireland if I saw some Protestant or Catholic bludgeon the life out of my wife when she innocently answered the knock on the front door. I might even have been a terrorist myself if I had existed for years in some refugee camp in the Gaza Strip with no prospect of a life of my own. The terrible truth is no one knows what he would do given sufficient provocation and sufficient deprivation. The wisest course for us first of all is not to opt out of the embarrassing diagnosis which the X-ray probe called the Cross of Christ reveals. Of course we are innocent of the sins of frightfulness such as we have listed, but we are not innocent of the raw material which produces it, and God knows to what level we might not stoop but for the fortunate circumstances which have constituted our protection.

And if ever there was a time in history over which the Cross stands in terrible judgement that surely is the present. We boast of our enlightened democracy, but was the Poulson affair only the tip of the iceberg?

4 *The healing purpose*

But come back to the analogy with which I began, the poultice acting on the man with the poisoned finger. It drew the poison to the surface and dispersed it. Could not this be a picture of the working of the Cross of Christ upon sinful humanity? It draws the poison to the surface. Yes, we see it gathered to a head in that ghastly incident called the crucifixion of Jesus, but it is drawn to the surface in order to be dispersed, in order that men shall be healed, or saved, if we prefer the old words, that is what Good Friday is about and that is what we need to take into our sights again. 'Jesus Christ, crucified for the world's salvation.'

2(b)   GOOD FRIDAY

God's healing love

> Romans 5. 8 'But God commendeth his love towards us, in that while we were yet sinners Christ died for us.'

1 *An act of love*

Now we must turn to the love of God. We must in fact turn to see the love of God at work in the crucifixion of Jesus Christ. And this at the outset and on any surface interpretation, sounds ridiculous. How could we see love in action in a scene where a man is being brutally murdered? A man who is innocent and not only innocent but godlike; indeed confessed to be the Son of God by those with the discernment of faith? Where fear, bloodlust, cruelty, callousness and contempt occupy a plot of ground dominated by a hillock so uglily shaped as to appear like a man's head stripped of all its flesh, and that hillock surmounted by three repulsive gibbets—how can anyone in his senses pontificate about the love of God, or the love of anyone else or indeed love at all, except as love trampled on till all its life is killed completely? And it has all happened before. Men have crucified men, sometimes in hundreds, good men, bad men, savages, saints. How in any of these offensive deaths can one hope to see the love of God? And the problem is not outdated. A month ago I received a pamphlet about life under the Communist system which pointed out how more Christians had died for their faith in the twentieth century than under the Roman Empire.

Yet this is where we have to plant our feet on Good Friday as we stand before the Cross of Christ. And when our service is over, if we are not still standing firmly in the love of God we shall have missed the message of this day. It would be easy to stand instead in a trough of depression, easy to pity ourselves as a generation caught in a trap of frightening financial inflation so that we do not know what life will hold for us in twelve months' time, easy to set up Christ's pain as a mirror of our pain and to stare at nothing in that event but a reflection of our own drawn faces and to slink away with nothing.

> 'Nothing in my hand I bring'
> And nothing at the end I take away.

Or if we sidestep the debilitating exercise of reflected self-pity, what notions shall we entertain of the nature of God if we do not firmly plant our feet on a recognition of his love?—A god of terror? A god of pitiless wrath? A god whose satisfaction it is to extract the last painful drop of blood from every one who rebels against his holy sovereignty, yes, even the blood of his son? What heathen thinking is this?—But so come all those repelling notions of those hideous theologies wherein Christ propitiated with blood, an angry Father, a god appeased, toned down, satisfied with human gore as if he were a kind of Shylock; notions of God and Christ set over against each other as opposites, one doing one thing, one another. Two gods of different natures, one avenging, one loving.

On top of all these misconceptions Paul wrote one convincing, shattering sentence—'God commendeth his love towards us, in that while we were yet sinners Christ died for us.' Everything about Good Friday issues from that love of God exhibited in Jesus Christ. This is the plot of ground on which we must plant our feet as we take up our stance before the Cross on Good Friday—the love of God in Jesus Christ.

2 *Love for the unworthy*

But why? Why do we need the love of God? Let me change the question. Why do we need anyone's love? I don't think I know, except that we do. A life without love in it is scarcely even life. What more terrible sentence could you pass on a man that he should die alone, unloved and forsaken. The truth is we shrivel without love, shrivel with the cold, too cold to exist. Everyone needs the warmth of someone's love. 'It is love that makes the world go round', *l'amor che move il sole e l'altre stelle*, wrote Dante in the last line of his Paradiso, 'It is love that moves the sun and the other stars.'

And what love is most worthy of the name? It is the love that knows all about us and still continues loving. Love which recognises that I have not always been faithful and yet does not turn against me. Love which has dragged through the hurting experience of being spurned, even ridiculed and lampooned, but yet goes on loving. The French novelist Jouhandeau in a story with the title *Cocu pendu et content* tells of a husband whose wife let him down terribly, but when she fell ill and became repulsive even to behold by means of her disease, he spared no expense to provide medical treatment, even nursing her himself, and when she died he followed her coffin down the village street to the shattered amazement of all peering through the windows, a man's love for an unlovely woman. Love operating through pain, that is the stature of divine love, that the stature of God's love of us. 'God commendeth his love towards us in that while we were yet sinners Christ died for us.'

3 *We are the unworthy*

But are we unworthy? Are we unworthy of God's love? Is the whole human race unworthy of God's love? What about that man in Londonderry recently who planted a bomb in a milk churn? What about that burglar who broke into the flat belonging to the Lady-in-waiting of Princess Anne in Chelsea, held her up and raped her? What about it? Yes, what about it? Aren't the papers full every-day of merciless deeds done mostly for greed, gain or political motives? And once again we cry, 'Include me out! I am no party to such deeds.' Nor are we! Let us be sensible. But what about our sins of omission? Do they not also make us unworthy? Have I not been the priest or the Levite who passed by on the other side? That man who appealed to me for help and I turned him down. That woman whom another woman could not find it in her heart to praise—is she not worse for that omission? Oh no, we aren't bad people, all we ever do is leave undone the things we might have done. But sins always spoil, they coarsen and they dwarf, even sins of omission. But God loves us all the same—that is the message, the astonishing message of Good Friday. 'God commendeth his love towards us, in that while we were yet sinners, Christ died for us.'

Yes, there are people who will sit down under this. But what about God's love for the property speculators, the traffickers in arms deals and the oppressors of the blacks in South Africa and other less glamorous places of the earth? They are sinners, yes, every young person today will label those as sinners, but what if the New Testament means that God loves these traffickers as well! Yes, loves even rich sinners, sinners with flats in Mayfair, and private suites at the Hilton. Can we, dare we, accept a God like this or a Christ like this? Or must he for a love like this be crucified to death?

What more is there to say? Who is there able to escape the judgement of love, the love which suffers, the love which loves the rich man, poor man, beggar-man, thief? We have nothing to say, we had better have nothing to say! 'There is a time to speak and a time to refrain from speaking' says the book of Proverbs, and the time to refrain is when we stand on the plot of ground before Christ's Cross. It dumbfounds us, baffles us. Why? Because it is love to the uttermost. God's love for the unworthy among whom I stand with no clothes but those of superficial respectability.

> *'When I survey the wondrous Cross*
> *On which the prince of glory died,*
> *My richest gain I count but loss,*
> *And pour contempt on all my pride.'*
> (I. Watts)

14

But when I am brought to the end of myself, when the world, the civilised world, the uncivilised world is brought to the end of itself, the star of hope can begin to rise, for man's extremity is God's opportunity.

2(c)   GOOD FRIDAY

One man's work

> 2 Corinthians 5. 19 (N.E.B.) '. . . *God was in Christ reconciling the world to himself, no longer holding men's misdeeds against them . . .*'

My guess is that there is one word in this text with which we shall not disagree. It is the word 'misdeeds.' The things that were done to Jesus at Calvary were 'misdeeds.' This surely is an understatement. But the text goes on to assert that God has rubbed out these misdeeds, they are cancelled, they are not, they will not, be held against us any more.

1 *Not a progress landmark*

And of course we approve. This is good. What is more, we reckon God reasonable to act in this way, because after all, we would never commit this kind of misdeed again. We would never convict an innocent person to preserve the status quo, and certainly never crucify anyone. We have been civilised beyond these barbarities . . . . Perhaps we have, but I doubt it. If, however, we do adopt this kind of mental stance before the Cross of Christ, viewing it as the kind of disgrace beyond which civilised man has progressed, I think we are entirely mistaken as to its purpose. The Cross does not stand as a kind of low water-mark in the story of mankind. For one thing it does not stand at the beginning of the story at all but a long way in. Man has been on the earth for, perhaps, five-hundred thousand years and the crucifixion of Christ occurred only two thousand years ago at a point when civilization had reached one of its peaks, the *Pax Romana*. What is more, the crucifixion of Christ was not carried out in some heathen outlandish society, in some geographical outback; Christ was crucified at Jerusalem, the Holy City, a place of worship of the true God. No, the Cross of Christ does not indicate how far we have progressed from our barbaric origins. It gives no credit to civilized man at all.

2 Not hopeful of environment

Nor does the Cross of Christ hold out much hope of environment as a reforming instrument. If our text is right in asserting that, 'God was in Christ reconciling the world to himself', then God made very little use of improved circumstances to accomplish his purposes. There is a smarting rub at this point, because we make so much of improved circumstances. We have been improving circumstances for all our worth since the second world war ended thirty years ago. Wages are up, living standards are up, facilities for education are up, opportunities for welfare and the maintenance of health are up. What isn't up when you come to assess the environment as compared with fifty years ago? We are quite sure that if only children are reared in a better environment they will improve far beyond the standards of their deprived parents. And if only adults have sufficient money they will give up stealing, dishonesty and the avoidance of hard work. Marriages will hold and families live happily together. Man is able to be redeemed by the improvement of his living conditions.

Put these two ideas together that man has progressed beyond the barbarities of an early age represented by the crucifixion of Christ, and man can be improved basically by improving his environment, and you have the philosophy of the mid-twentieth century still passionately held by thousands of people.

3 No use made of the good in either man or his environment

But if God was reconciling man to himself at Calvary, at the Cross of Christ, he does not seem to have made use of this philosophy at all. No one comes out of the crucifixion story with any medals. Even the apostles forsook their master and fled, one a traitor, another denied him, and there isn't much difference. God puts very little trust in man to improve himself, except superficially. And as for the environment, what could be more of a write-off than a place of crucifixion? Everything about it was obscene. There was no civilised activity in the entire scene except perhaps the jar of drugged wine made available for the crucified victims to help kill the pain—that was all. God apparently used nothing of the good in man and nothing of the good in the environment as instruments with which to carry out his plan of reconciling man to himself. All he used was an individual, one lone man who walked the road alone to the place of his execution.

4 *God used an individual*

It is as well first of all to observe this fact at its surface level. Everyone had forsaken Jesus. Where were the crowds that hung on his words in Galilee, proud to own him as their prophet? They were not there taking any part in his defence! Where were the disciples who had committed their lives to him and whom he counted as his closest friends? They had made good their escape and were in hiding, probably behind closed doors in the city! Where was even one volunteer to carry his cross to the place of torture, lessening at least that load for the last procession? There was not even one! For Simon of Cyrene was press-ganged into playing that part. What Christ did at Calvary he did absolutely alone.

This puts the whole weight of what God was doing in the event on to an individual. This is not easy for us to accept in our democratic way of life. Individuals are not what we see as proper instruments for the improvement of society, but committees, majority decisions. We fuss and fuss about experts and spend enormous sums of money on educating them to be experts but when decisions have to be taken, we call for a referendum, every one must have his say whether he knows anything about the subject or not. Democracy is all but worshipped. But when God set about redeeming the world, he did it with an individual whom every one voted down, 'crucify him.'

Perhaps, if the Cross of Christ does no more for us than this— warn us to set limits to our democratic procedures, and to give more weight to what individuals can do in creative work, in redeeming work, and in revealing the truth of life, it will be something.

5 *God's sole action*

Even so we have not reached the heart of the matter. The Cross is not merely a class-room lesson for democracy, the Cross of Christ is God's action. It is God's action for the reconciliation of men. It is God's action for the reconciliation of men by no longer holding man's misdeeds against them. In this whole business no credit is given to man at all. Everything, everything in the whole affair of

God reconciling man to himself has its initiative with God himself. Starkly this is what the Cross asserts.

But what does it mean? Let us get to the point. What does it mean—God reconciles us to himself by no longer holding our misdeeds against us? Does it mean that once we see how kind, how good, how gracious God is, that we shall then reform ourselves and be much improved in consequence? Is this how you read human nature?

6 God's removal of barriers

Surely God is no fool. What then does the reconciliation mean? It means that God has taken down the barriers we have erected by our misdeeds between ourselves and him. None of them will be counted against us. We can go straight into God's presence, if we will, because he has come straight into ours, of his will.

All this is so different from the attitude of mind which reckons that man can outbalance his misdeeds by his good deeds, and so offer God a moral credit card. 'Look, God, I know I did this and that and the other, and I am sorry, but look, I have also done this and that and the other and I want to suggest that my account is now straight.' (I've done it myself.) 'So you will accept me, won't you?' This approach has nothing to do with the gospel of God's grace. It is the gospel of good works which is no gospel at all because half of us do not know what misdeeds we have done or what even comprises misdeeds. We get blinded by our misdeeds and even if we half see them we spend our time in self-justification. No, this credit scheme with God is useless. The only way of safety is God's act of reconciliation through Christ whereby he no longer holds our misdeeds against us. And the proper response is thanksgiving.

'God was in Christ reconciling . . .' Yes, one lone man was the means. One lone man carried through the work. One lone man carried the burden. One lone man paid the price. One lone man made the sacrifice of himself which a work of this stature demands. We must not think of being at one with God apart from that lone man. He is 'the way, the truth and the life,' or to put the case in the shortest, most concise sentence, 'Christ is our salvation.'

Liberation

Psalm 126. 1, 2

> '*When the Lord turned again the captivity of Sion:*
> *then were we like unto them that dream.*
> *Then was our mouth filled with laughter:*
> *and our tongue with joy.*'

The Bible of the early Church was the Old Testament, for when it began, no New Testament existed. Christian congregations, therefore, would have no difficulty in applying the words of Psalm 126 to the resurrection of Jesus Christ. This was the great event which, like the return of the Jewish people from exile in Babylon in the sixth century B.C. set men free. And freedom following on captivity is unbelievable, almost dream-like, joy spills over into laughter, and laughter into joy.

1 *Exodus*

There is another reason why a comparison of the resurrection of Christ with the return from exile is appropriate. That return was counted as Israel's second exodus. The first exodus was the deliverance from the slavery in Egypt under the leadership of Moses. This stupendous event never ceased to dominate Israel's history and was the ground event of her theology, even the key to her laws.

> '*I am the Lord thy God, which brought thee up out of the land of Egypt, out of the house of bondage. Thou shalt have no other gods before me.*' (Exodus 20. 2,3)

Egypt then, and the deliverance from Egypt, runs like a thread throughout the whole Old Testament. There are songs about it, poems about it, prophetic words about it, legal enactments about it, ceremonies built on it and instructions to future generations how to keep it always in remembrance. And when the early Church came to interpret the earth-shaking event which was the ground of its being, namely, the resurrection of Jesus on Easter Day, it did so in terms of the deliverance from Egypt.

Exodus, then, that is, 'way out', is the key word of the Bible. There is the exodus from Egypt, the exodus from Babylon and the exodus from the grave by Jesus Christ on Easter Day. And always the sequel was joy and thanksgiving. In Exodus 15 'Then sang

Moses and the children of Israel this song unto the Lord, and spake, saying, "I will sing unto the Lord, for he hath triumphed gloriously:" ' And in Psalm 126:

> *When the Lord turned again the captivity of Sion:*
> *then were we like unto them that dream.*
> *Then was our mouth filled with laughter:*
> *and our tongue with joy.*'

And in our Church hymn book down the centuries:

> '*We hymn thee rising from the grave,*
> *From death returning strong to save;*
> *Thine own right hand the tyrant chains,*
> *And paradise for man regains.*'

2 The human predicament

But some one wants to ask, 'Isn't this overdone?' Granted a people can enter into the exhilaration of a nation's deliverance from foreign oppression. Granted joy can be overwhelming when the prison gates for a whole community are flung wide open and the captives freed. Anyone who saw the television presentation of Colditz will remember vividly the day when the American forces reached that prison camp and the forbidding iron gates were unlocked for ever. Men entered into these situations physically. But what are we to say about the resurrection of Jesus from the grave on Easter Day two thousand years ago? How can it appeal to me? How can it affect me? How can you possibly expect me to sing about it?

> '*When the Lord turned again the captivity of Sion:*
> *then were we like unto them that dream.*
> *Then was our mouth filled with laughter:*
> *and our tongue with joy.*'

Isn't this overdone?

It is not overdone if you are at all aware of man's plight. Man is a captive. Man is an exile. The really terrifying fact of modern existence is that man is the prisoner of his own technological expertise. The money system he has devised has caught him in a net of inflation from which no government yet has found the way of escape. The processes of industrialization have flooded the earth with goods till we are in danger altogether of exhausting its resources. And most sombre of all is the unrelieved watch round the clock from a 'nerve centre' deep down in the ground in America's Middle West, and an aeroplane up in the skies ready to launch nuclear rockets from any one of the forty-three nuclear sites around the globe, each rocket delivering a weight of explosives equivalent to the total of conventional bombs dropped in World War II. It is to this brink of disaster man's cleverness has brought him, and all, let it not be forgotten, with an aim of averting, not waging, total war. This is the gigantic size of the human tragedy, and this is the devastating poignancy, that man's laudable efforts bring frightening consequences, and ideals like the United Nations Council and the Welfare State run aground with the passage of time.

All this makes the human race feel like some exile on this planet. The winds and waves belong, the mountains and hills, the valleys beneath, and the depths of the sea, and what inhabits them, but man seems doomed to blank frustration, living out his little life of seventy years or more, shorter by far than the products of his own devising, half happy, half wretched, knowing that in the end the forces of nature will push him off the scene whatever he achieves. Man is not at home but 'a stranger and a sojourner as all his fathers were', a homelessness none have expressed more poignantly than the poets, and among them none more than the exiled Heinrich Heine, of Jewish origin:

> *Ich hatte einst ein schönes Vaterland*
> *Der Eichenbaum*
> *Wuchs dort so hoch, die Veilchennickten sanft*
> *Es war ein Traum*

And among twentieth century men it is the Frenchman Jean Paul Sartre that has described most vividly the meaninglessness of life as we experience it.

It is when we begin to sense the predicament of man in depth like this that we see how no surface thinking can set the problem right. We may go off on some binge, drown ourselves in work or pleasure according (as some scientists would say) to what our genes determine for us, we may return to the pagan gods of sex and Bacchus, attempting to dignify them with every kind of name and philosophy, but in the end nothing can answer the two ultimate questions—is death the end of all, and if it is, how do we rid the world of pointlessness?

3 The deliverance

It is here that Easter Day dawns with its message, 'The Lord is risen indeed and has appeared unto Simon' (Luke 24. 34). At first these words seem 'way-out' and totally irrelevant. But that is precisely why they are significant. They come from another dimension. They derive from outside the historic chain of cause and effect. They constitute an inrush into human existence of something different. At least in this Karl Barth was right, nothing but action from outside can save us, and this is what Easter Day declares has happened.

Please note the tense, 'has happened.' What we have to declare is not first a philosophy, but something that occurred at a particular time and at a particular place. Christ rose from the dead. This is not an event that can be explained away. If that were possible disbelievers would have accomplished it long since. But the remarkable fact is that the stream of books about the resurrection of Christ from the dead has continued in fuller spate than ever this last decade and still the statement stands there for discussion. It is exceedingly tough!

But consider the phrase more closely. 'The Lord is risen indeed and has appeared unto Simon.' The resurrection of Christ is not only an historical event, it is a present experience. 'The Lord is risen—the Lord has appeared.' Simon was an ordinary man. The fact that he is called Simon here and not Peter, and certainly not St Peter, emphasises the fact. So the appearance of the risen Christ to him suggests the truth that this historical event is something which breaks through into the personal experience of ordinary people. And in this the controversial German theologian Bultmann was also right, the resurrection of Christ must bear a meaning to us personally if it is to bear much meaning at all. Christ has, however, broken through my prison wall, the prison wall of the ultimate deadendness of life and therefore of my deadendness. He has set us free. He has accomplished our exodus. He has brought us home from exile. And when the abolition of death means the abolition of pointlessness, we can face the tangled problems of our human predicament because there is *value in the struggle*, value to be realised beyond the margins of the temporal.

God help us if we are so 'slow of heart' (Luke 24. 25) to grasp the implication of Christ's resurrection and to accept the liberation which it offers. Liberation from pointlessness. Liberation from fear. Liberation from crippling self-centredness. Liberation by faith into God's purpose for mankind, lifting up our personalities into a new found buoyancy.

> '*When the Lord turned again the captivity of Sion:*
> *then were we like unto them that dream.*
> *Then was our mouth filled with laughter:*
> *and our tongue with joy.*'

4   WHITSUNDAY

The waiting room
Luke 24. 49 (N.E.B.) '... *Stay here in this city until* ...'

Everyone is familiar with a waiting room. There is the waiting room at the dentist's where you sit wondering if you need have come because the pain seems to have disappeared since your arrival. There is the station waiting room, perhaps, on some exposed site like Colwyn Bay or Chalkwell Bay, where in winter the tiny bunch of travellers huddle round a feeble radiator, hoping against hope that the train will not be late. Or the plush waiting room at Heathrow Airport from which no passengers can move till they are called. Or the up-to-date variety of this at Dulles Airport, Washington D.C. where the whole lounge, passengers and all, moves out to the aircraft itself. Not even in our faster-than-sound modern travel is the waiting room outmoded. Indeed, those who journey by air seem to spend as much time waiting as in moving. It is a strange fact about life in general, that for all our speed, we still have to wait, and because of the speed modern man finds the waiting especially frustrating.

1 *The Apostolic waiting room*
Did it ever occur to you that the place in which the few followers of Jesus Christ were assembled on the first Whitsunday was a waiting room? They had been waiting, according to St Luke, for at least ten days, and if not in one room, certainly in one city, never out of contact, never out of call. We can guess they found the waiting difficult. Good Friday had been gloriously reversed by the

stupendous rising of their crucified Lord from the grave. What is more, this risen Christ had actually appeared to more than one of his followers and the whole Apostolic company together, assuring them of his 'aliveness' for evermore. Why not 'get on with the job'? Why not rush up the steps of the Praetorium and hammer on Pilate's door crying, 'You've made a mistake! We've seen Jesus of Nazareth, the man you condemned to death!' Would not a public statement from the Procurator's palace be the proper way to promote the Christian cause? After all, a movement needs influence, it needs backing. And why not parade up and down outside Caiaphas's lodging in a protest march, 'Annas out! Caiaphas out! The Sanhedrin out!' Ten thousand Galileans would surely rally to the support of their man from Galilee. But no! The Apostles were told to wait. 'You must wait,' said the risen Christ, 'for the promise made by the Father about which you heard me speak.' And so they waited. How they must have chafed! It is true they did set about holding an election to fill the empty place made by the defection of Judas, but whether this action was right and whether they ought to have used the casting of lots as part of their method, it is hard to say. It looks as if Saul of Tarsus and not Matthias was the man to fill the vacancy. However, on the whole, the followers of Jesus did as they were told, they 'stuck it out' in the waiting room.

Then it happened, all of a sudden. They were actually together at that moment in a room. Was it the Upper Room where the Lord's supper had taken place? We do not know. But all at once clothes, hangings and parchments seemed to be blown backwards and forwards in a strong, driving wind. They could hear it gusting along in the street outside. Doors and shutters rattled. What was more, the room seemed to be abnormally lit by tongues like flames of fire. Imagination? No, not imagination. Symbolism then? Yes, may-be symbolism but reality all the same. This was the Spirit starting the Christian mission in the world. It was for this that the followers of Jesus had to wait sitting in the waiting room.

2 The abolition of the waiting room

And ever since that first Whitsunday Christians have made a mistake over and over again, they have thought they could abolish the waiting room. Yes, even with the book of the Acts of the Apostles in their hands they have thought so. It is as if St Luke had never told us that while the Christians in Antioch were keeping a fast and offering worship to the Lord (that is, waiting) the Holy

Spirit said, 'Set Barnabas and Saul apart for me, to do the work to which I have called them.' (Acts 13. 2) It was as if St Luke had had never written it down in sober historical narrative (Acts 13. 4), how 'these two, sent out on their mission by the Holy Spirit, came down to Seleucia, and from there sailed to Cyprus.' And how in Acts 16. 6, these men 'were prevented by the Holy Spirit from delivering the message in the province of Asia.'

These members of the early Church were the Sons of God, not because they were paragons of virtue—Paul and Barnabas fell out after a quarrel—but because they chose to be led by the Spirit. 'As many as are led by the Spirit of God, they are the sons of God' wrote St Paul in his letter to the Romans. Their own disciples and their own Lord, told these men that the Spirit would lead them and guide them and they believed what they heard and acted upon it. This is the reason for the success of the Church mission recorded in the book of the Acts of the Apostles. They were Apostles led by the Spirit.

3 The re-instatement of the waiting room

And what about the Church today? Is it fair to ask if we have not substituted the Committee Room for the Waiting Room? The statistical unit for the praying unit? It is easy to cast stones at the Established Church but those who do had better examine first how eager they are to plan their own lives, and to protest when things do not work out according to their own predelictions and what they reckon as their rights.

In the nineteenth century there was a famous Calvinist preacher in Paris called Adolphe Monod, who drew large crowds to listen to his sermons. He fell ill, however, with an incurable disease which confined him to his bed until he died. During those months, however, he gave short addresses to a select few who gathered round his bed, and someone had the foresight to take copious notes so that the talks were subsequently published. It was on January 13th 1856 that he described how we often make excellent plans for our lives intending to carry out the loftiest ideals and accomplish the most diligent work, but they are *our* plans, and self is in the centre. 'This is the work I intend to do', and the results are meagre, because they never were God's plans for us. We can spend too much time in making plans. It is better to remain in the waiting room until God's plans appear, and these are shown by circumstances. If each day is mixed with constant prayer, the day itself will declare what we ought to do. This will be God's will and bear God's enrichment. So much will be accomplished.

In one of his broadcast talks Archbishop Anthony Bloom said the Church should be like an English sheep dog. He does not move till he receives the signal from his master, but as soon as he does he goes 'all out', wagging his tail all the time.

This is the proper proportion of waiting and working. Waiting for the leading of the Spirit, working with the power of the Spirit.

Has the modern Church a waiting room in its impressive structure? If not, of what use the structure? Has the modern Christian a waiting room in activism? If not, what price his good works? The wind blows where it wills. No one can make it blow. The Spirit works where he will. The only sensible course is to wait for it, like a sailing ship at anchor, and then, as soon as there is a flapping at the mast-head, make for the open sea, or to change the metaphor back to the phrase from St Luke 24. 49: '... stay here in this city until ....'

5   HARVEST THANKSGIVING

Gratitude

> Luke 17. 17 *'Were there not ten cleansed? But where are the nine?'*

In one of the London Art Galleries, there hangs a picture, the subject of which derives from the first world war and the first surprise gas attack. A long line of blinded British soldiers, each with his hands on the shoulders of the man in front, every one blind except the one leading them back to base. It is a picture which haunts you. You can't get it out of your mind's eye.

1 *The appeal of ten*

Today I bring to your notice a similar picture from the New Testament, a gang of ten men, all lepers, clinging together because the deficiencies of one might be compensated by the faculties of another; the man without hands helped by the one who still possessed them. A terrible picture, a moving refuse heap of human dereliction, but a reminder of the all but endless line of pitiable refugees, emaciated, diseased and half demented, who shuffle along east of Suez today outside Europe's affluence.

But somehow news filtered through to these ten lepers that one lone leper somewhere had been healed by Jesus of Nazareth. And so when the opportunity arose they decided they would put their case. So we see them standing afar off calling out their pitiable *eleison* as Jesus crossed the lonely frontier between Galilee and Samaria, the only kind of lonely living space lepers could occupy. 'Jesus, Master, take pity on us.'

There is something daunting about seeing one sufferer with only half a body but enough to bend the mind when you see them in rows. Such is the story of the world's suffering, the very scale of the tragedy. Today on our Harvest Thanksgiving Sunday a large percentage of the world's population exist below starvation level. It is the massiveness which hurts.

In this story, Jesus answered the call of rudimentary faith, as he always does, but in a strange way. He called to them, 'Go, show yourselves to the priests' (who were of course the Medical Officers of Health of the day), the very officials these lepers with good reason avoided. And stranger still, they set off on the road, ten shuffling lepers, dragging and pushing those whose legs had long since ceased to function. And then it happened. Somewhere on that road it happened. 'Look, my hands! I can move them. My feet! My feet! I feel as if I could run.' And they all with dancing eyes that never had danced since they were children, if even then, declared that the torpor and the numbness characteristic of the disease had seeped quite clean away from every leprous limb and they were whole.

Some time ago there stood in Cook's Travel Agency in Kensington High Street an old lady almost blind. A friend stood behind to hold her up and guide her hand to sign her travel documents. Her destination was Lourdes, and when the formalities were finished she made one short revealing remark which left the man behind the counter speechless. 'I hope this time I shall be able to see when I return.'

Perhaps she can by now, who knows? But in all matters of personal need, be it blindness, boredom, meaninglessness, anxiety or fear, the one right course of action is to do the thing which spells obedience. In this case, 'Go, show yourselves to the priests. And it came to pass as they went they were cleansed.' Too many people negatively complain, too few positively act.

Then what? Look down the road. Ten lepers dancing! Is that what you see? Ten lepers banding together arm in arm! This time, no leader necessary, for no leprous limbs existed needing compensation by the one still whole. 'Come, let us find our healer. Let us sing his praises. Let us do all we can in sheer abundant gratitude.' Is this what we see?

Not in this picture, and remember, it is a mirror of mankind. You see one man returning to render thanks. One man ... 'Were there not ten cleansed? But where are the nine?' The facts are that ninety-per-cent gave no thanksgiving. Only one man and he was a foreigner, a man with slight pigmented skin.

What happened to the others? Why did not they all come back? Why was there no word of thanks upon their lips? Perhaps they thought good health was their right. God ought never to have let them be in trouble. It was not charity they wanted, but justice, decent human justice. We hear that cry today. We hear it often.

Perhaps they had other pressing engagements. Perhaps some shop somewhere in some bazaar they'd had to leave when their leprosy was obvious demanded their attention. No time for religion. The shop! For us, maybe, it is the car to be washed on Sunday mornings and the social contacts. These could be reasons.

And some one complains—'What have I, anyway, to thank God for? I had little holiday this year. It rained. The rent of my flat has been increased. The traffic on the roads has taken all the fun out of motoring ...'

I suggest we should first thank God for the historic faith. How is it life is not meaningless to you, but is meaningless to the man whose only hope is in marihuana and after that, the bottle?

I suggest you should be thankful for the fact that you are here this morning, able to walk, able to see, able even to sing a bit, though maybe out of tune (which doesn't matter).

I suggest the fact of the meal that awaits us when we reach home and the gifts of harvests of the earth reaching our tables when many millions can only pick out scraps from other people's dustbins, are causes for thankfulness.

What have I got to thank God for? In God's name what?

One leper came back to prostrate himself at Jesus' feet giving him thanks. Was that excessive? We don't like enthusiasm in our northern brand of religious devotion. But it could be real, it could be practical. We could do something today as an expression of gratitude. I am asking for gifts. Not for the Church this time. I am asking you to help feed those who are hungry. I am asking you to give, yes, to give money for their needs . . .

Were there not ten cleansed? Where are the nine? O Lord, I forgot all about it. O Lord, I had to take the dog out. O Lord, I was up late the night before . . .

Were there not ten cleansed? Where are the nine? One returned giving his thanks. Will that be you? Only you can tell.

6   REMEMBRANCE SUNDAY

God's memory

Psalm 112. 6 '*The righteous shall be had in everlasting remembrance.*'

Introduction

Do you think they will? You who read the daily newspapers and especially the Sunday papers, do you think the righteous will be had in everlasting remembrance? Apart from the obituary notices they do not receive many inches in the press! If a man is a public figure and spends time visiting old people in their homes, there are no headlines. We do not hear about it on the eight o'clock news; but let him be caught in a drug racket and the press men bring out the biggest type. Evil deeds receive the most coverage. Evil men remain longest in the memory, Rasputin, Eichman, Jack the Ripper. Who remembers now the train driver who was beaten to his knees in the cab of his engine by the great train robbers and has since died because of his injuries? But everyone knows Biggs and Mrs Biggs. We are told that she has been paid thirty thousand pounds for her story and may live in peace in Australia. 'The righteous shall be had in everlasting remembrance.' Is this verse from the Psalms true, or is it only wishful thinking?

1 *Wishful thinking*

That 'the righteous ought to be had in everlasting remembrance' is wishful thinking. It is more than wishful thinking, but it is at

29

least that. We do wish, all of us, deep down inside us, that the righteous were had in everlasting remembrance. We think they ought to be and are sorry if they are not.

At a School Speech Day recently a Headmaster was lamenting the fact that some parents of the boys were only too willing to let their children do jobs in the evenings and throughout the holidays with the result that lower academic results were obtained than would otherwise have been the case. He asserted that the parents were jeopardising their sons' future for the sake of easy money now, all of which comment was received in stony silence by both parents and boys. Present material gain was what seemed to matter to them. Later on, however, he had occasion to mention one boy whose academic achievement was disappointing, though not through lack of ability. The reason was the boy was busy three nights a week helping to decorate old people's rooms free of charge. Instantly the whole audience, when they heard, broke into a clap.

This is my point, we feel in our bones, we know, that goodness deserves recognition and should receive it. The righteous ought to be had in everlasting remembrance.

2 Our memorials

Because we have this innate conviction that 'the righteous ought to be had in everlasting remembrance', we have our war memorials. It is why we have the Unknown Warrior's Grave in Westminster Abbey. An army Chaplain, the Reverend David Railton M.C., first suggested it. He was so impressed with the fact that many men had done brave deeds in the war where no one saw them, and in consequence had no recognition, no decorations, no medals, that something ought to be done to keep them in remembrance. And so some unknown soldier's body was wrapped in a Union Jack and re-buried in the Abbey, our national shrine of greatest honour. And so right was this felt to be that it was copied by the Americans at the *National Cemetery* at Arlington and by the French at the *Arc de Triomphe* in Paris and the *Chiesa di Santa Maria degli Angeli* in Rome for the Italians. All feel that the righteous, even the unknown righteous, should be had in everlasting remembrance.

But what happens as the years roll away? For how long will the annual ceremony take place in the Albert Hall, London? For how many years will a service be conducted at the Cenotaph? Let us be careful. Let us not sweep away too many old landmarks too soon. It is doubtful whether the gain is as great as the loss. Things are not bad because they are old. Things are not good because they are new. The worst that can happen because of the changes is that people should feel they are forgotten. For as long as there is one person alive for whom life was utterly broken by the wars, for his sake, for her sake, it could be right that this landmark called Remembrance Sunday should stand.

3 God's memory

Yet the time must eventually come when the wars we remember today will be as remote as the Crimean War is to us, and a red poppy will no longer evoke memories as it does today. What then? Are the righteous still had in everlasting remembrance? The Church will answer with a firm 'yes' because it has always believed that there exists apart from your mind and my mind, and everybody else's mind, an Eternal mind, whom we call God, and it is there finally that the righteous are had in everlasting remembrance.

Of course there are difficulties in this faith. Of course it is precisely these twentieth-century wars that have caused many people to lose their faith. They ask, 'How can the presence of evil be compatible with a God of love?' Or more subtly, as regards the removal of evil from the world, either God cannot or he will not. If he cannot, he is not almighty, if he will not, he cannot be good.

We can, however, and we must point to the historical Jesus. He was crucified. This was an evil. There is always that in men which reacts to beauty with the will to destroy it. But Jesus rose from the dead. This is the heart of the gospel. Death was not, death is not, the end. Evil was not, is not, the last word. So by means of the Cross and Resurrection of Christ the conviction grew, and has held, that evil does not cancel out God, but that God in the end will cancel out evil. What happened to Christ is the evidence. So in spite of the evil, no, because of the way God in Christ triumphed over the evil, go on believing in God and keep the landmarks as a witness that 'the righteous shall be had in everlasting remembrance.'

More important still, do not feel ashamed to find comfort in this message, it is grounded in our faith in God and our faith in God is grounded both in history and in experience. God does not forget us. He never will. And we should not forget each other.

Salvation by belonging

During the years before the last war a little Russian girl grew up in Germany because her father was a priest there of the Russian Orthodox Church. She was happy, she loved Germany and went to school with little German girls of her own age, even coming to enjoy the scripture lessons in the strict Lutheran tradition. Then hostilities broke out and in time war with Russia. Was happiness possible now for the little Russian? Was it possible when the British forces crossed the Rhine and treated her as a German! Could there be any happiness when, bereft of her family she was despatched to Holland, officially listed as 'stateless'! No country wanted this girl. She belonged nowhere and to no one. Finally, however, fortune turned and she found herself in England. And then the greatest benefaction of all came, which no one can appreciate who has never known what it feels like to be stateless she was granted a British passport. At last she belonged. From tha' moment she began to develop as a person.

1 *On behalf of this child*

Our service today is a very happy occasion. It is good to see you all here and to welcome you—family, relations, friends, and of course, the baby, the smallest, youngest and (in a way) most insignificant of us all, but for whose welfare we have in fact assembled. Did I say 'welfare'? Yes, I meant 'welfare.' We have come to this service for this child's good. I intend to express it even more strongly, for this child's 'wholeness', for this child's 'salvation.' When I put it like that you will see what an important occasion this is and how much you have already done by arranging to be present.

Now let us suppose for a moment that you had not come. Let us suppose that you had said among yourselves, 'Oh, it's rather a fuss getting all the relations together, and we are not sure whether all our friends would appreciate being invited to a church, and anyway, perhaps baptism isn't all that important in this scientific and technological age.' Would this little baby be left outside the love of God? Would you yourselves, all of you, be outside the concern of God? No, certainly not. God is like parents who can never forget their child, always their heart is towards him. God never moves away from us, but we can move away from him, and because we haven't today, but have assembled for this service, I want to stress what an important and happy occasion this is—dare I say it?—happy even for God!

2 Behaviour, believing and belonging

Now why is baptism important? Because it gives us the opportunity of salvation by belonging. There is a very ill-informed but widespread idea in existence that salvation comes to us by behaviour. We all of us accomplish some good in life and some ill, but if the good exceeds the ill, we shall pass, our salvation is assured. But what confidence can this provide! Moreover, such thinking is a travesty of the gospel of Christ. Much more secure is the conviction that our salvation is given us by way of our belief in Christ living, dying and being raised to life again on our behalf. Our beliefs, however, that is to say, our faith, is not as constant as unquestionably it should be. It wavers. It rises and falls. It shines brightly at times and at other times it is almost completely clouded over. And all because we are only human after all. Moreover, faith is an abstract thing. We cannot see it with our eyes, nor get our fingers round it. And so in his infinite compassion God offers us another way which is not contrary to faith, but incorporates faith. We may call it salvation by belonging, belonging to the company of his people.

3 Salvation temporal and eternal

When in a few minutes I shall take this little child in my arms, he will be named, and with that name be received into the body of Christ's Church. From that moment he will belong. He will belong to the company of God's people whose eternal destiny is assured. 'Christ loved the Church' said St Paul, 'loving and cherishing it even as his own flesh.' What could be more simple? What could be more plain? Salvation by belonging to the people whose salvation, for all their faults, God has promised.

Come back in thought with me to the story of the little stateless girl with which I began. Everything about her life changed when she knew she belonged, and when she held in her hands, as a young woman, her own passport. True, it was only a piece of cardboard, a photograph and some signatures, but it symbolised a new status for her and with the status a new dignity which had its effect on her person. She belonged. She was wanted. She had a recognised place. She possessed significance.

This baptism today is a simple affair, but it carries with it enormous consequences. By means of this symbol, sign and sacrament this child will henceforth belong, and by belonging will reap the benefits of belonging, which benefits are both psychological and spiritual, temporal and eternal. I appeal to you parents and godparents, see that as this child grows up he knows that he belongs, belongs to Christ's Church and that he is led to the point of faith for himself. Then his belonging can be confirmed and he can take his part as an adult member of Christ's Church owned by God, not for its goodness, but through his own infinite goodness and mercy.

8 THE EVE OF CONFIRMATION

Learning and living

> 2 Timothy 1. 13 (N.E.B.) *'Keep before you an outline of the sound teaching which you heard from me, living by the faith and love which are ours in Christ Jesus.'*

Tomorrow will be the day of your confirmation to which you have been looking forward for so long. No words of mine can take the place of the words of the Bishop who will confirm you, because he will be acting in the name of the whole Church. Through his prayers and the prayers of the assembled congregation, together with your own openness to the presence of God, there will come that strengthening by the Spirit of God which you will need in order to live out the new position you will have acquired as confirmed Christians.

Your actual confirmation will also mark, however, the end of your period of intensive preparation, and so there is every reason why this should be registered with a short address or charge from me your teacher. And this I can do no better than to construct on the basis of the words of an older man to a young man as set out in St Paul's second letter to Timothy—'Keep before you an outline of the sound teaching which you heard from me, living by the faith and love which are ours in Christ Jesus.'

1 Learning

'Keep before you an outline . . .' During these last weeks, extending over months, you have been given something. Do remember this. To some extent we are given our faith, we do not construct it all ourselves from nothing. It is true that in time as you grow older and enter into all kinds of experiences—love, disappointment, a demanding job, success, perhaps, and heartbreaking sorrow—you will come to fill out the faith you have been given with your own meaning and perhaps with modifications and enrichments, but all the developments will be on the basis of what you have been given. There is no sadder spectacle than to see a man in later life unable to gain the faith by which he observes others to be living but is unable to grasp it himself because he has nothing on which to build. I remember one such man, a scientist, walking up and down in my study, wringing his hands because the body of his son, a teenager, had just been recovered from the railway line, and he had no idea where to turn for consolation of any kind. He had never been given a faith of any sort. So hold firmly on to what you have received in these confirmation classes. Some of its meaning you already appreciate, but as with any masterpiece whether of music or of painting, you will come to appreciate fresh points in it as time goes on. 'Keep before you an outline of the sound teaching you have heard from me.'

2 Living

You will notice, however, how Paul continues 'living by the faith and love which are ours in Christ Jesus. It is that word 'living' that must be emphasised. Being a Christian is not primarily knowing a set of answers to a set of life's problems. Knowledge is important. It is not for nothing that Our Lord's followers were called 'disciples', that is, learners. Indeed, we Christians, as long as we live could always wear a large 'L' pinned to our persons, back and front. We are always learning more of God, ourselves and their relationship together. Head knowledge, book-learning and examinations are not, however, the primary factors in being a confirmed Christian. We can know a great many answers theoretically but be lamentable failures as Christians because we do not live out our discipleship in action. Paul bade Timothy live 'by the faith and love which are ours in Christ Jesus'. Here the word 'love' is prominent. A Christian who lives by his faith is one who is motivated by love. He cares about other people, this includes his family circle at home as well as the down-trodden blacks in South Africa. It means having a concern for the rich as well as the poor, it even embraces people whom we find trying, difficult or even hostile.

Notice how Paul writes, 'living by the faith and love which *are ours* in Christ Jesus.' No proper Christian teacher ever claims that the faith is his own peculiar possession, nor does it belong exclusively to those who are taught. We share the faith together, it is ours together, and we only have it at all because we all stand side by side in a circle around Jesus Christ as we shall soon be doing when we come together in the Holy Communion after the confirmation.

I admit it to be a hard faith which is laid upon you. The world is never wholly favourable to the Christian way of life, and none of us has sufficient resources in himself to succeed. But we believe in the grace of God, freely given to those who seek it by faith and obedience, by prayer and sacrament and with that enabling power we shall set a good example as confirmed Christian men and women in our day and generation. God grant this may be so.

9   A WEDDING

The garden called marriage

    1 Timothy 6. 20 (N.E.B.) '... *keep safe that which has been entrusted to you.*'

In the county of Wiltshire there are open to the public in the summer months at a tiny place called Stourton, the magnificent gardens of the eighteenth century Stourhead House. Perhaps you have seen them, if so, you will understand at once on what a high plane I place marriage when at this wedding service I liken it to those superb grounds.

1 *A gift*
The first fact that arrests the sightseers of those gardens is their glorious setting. They are set in a shallow hollow surrounded by gentle slopes, and through the valley there flows a full stream, feeding a spacious lake graced by swans. And the massive trees,

trees of various species, some from intriguing far-away places, indicate the astonishing fertility of the soil that is able to support them. All this the beholder at once recognises as given. No land-scape gardener was responsible for this aspect of those gardens. He used what nature provided. This setting was a gift from nature waiting to be used.

There is in marriage this aspect of givenness. Love comes to two people. They do not make it, and if they try they fail. Proust once said of a particular man, 'Like every one who is *not* in love, he imagined that one chose the person whom one loved after endless deliberations and on the strength of various qualities and advantages.' This is not true. Love hits you, and if it doesn't, what you experience is not love. In his first letter in the New Testament John wrote some striking words. He said, 'Love is from God.' This is why I am comparing marriage to those lovely gardens at Stour-head, they are only possible, true marriage is only possible, because of what is a pure gift of nature and of God. If we recognise this we shall treat marriage with the reverence it deserves. It is a precious gift God offers to some people. The first right reaction is to be profoundly grateful, and never, especially in the years to come, when custom replaces novelty, never to take your marriage for granted. God has given you something wonderful.

2 The work required

When, however, the visitor thinks about those spacious gardens, and the imitation Greek temple at the head of the lake, and the way the paths are made to curve around its banks so that ever and again the walker is granted new and unexpected vistas of its loveli-ness, it dawns upon him that a great deal of man's labour and man's ingenuity must have been expended in order to achieve the magnificence before his eyes.

And this also is true of married life. A successful marriage does not only descend from heaven, it is worked at by both partners. Husband and wife must try to understand each other. They must understand how their needs differ, and how they can be comple-mentary to each other. The woman may, by means of her intuition, be quicker to think herself into 'the man's shoes', but the man may be able, by rational thought, to analyse a situation more accurately and act accordingly. A woman is happier when she is wanted. A man is happier when he thinks he is self-sufficient. A happy marriage does not come about without working at thoughts

37

like these, and not only thinking about them but acting upon them. In five years' time it would be worth asking this question—What are you actually doing for each others' contentment now? This then is my second point. You must work at your garden called marriage.

3 *The protection needed*

One final observation, and once again beginning with those gardens. They have to be fenced. There is a way in, of course, but only by means of payment which constitutes the permission, otherwise the gardens would soon become a shambles. Quickly they would develop into a camping site or a car park, both of which may perform useful functions but not in that particular place.

You will have to protect your marriage and I am not thinking solely of either partner being seduced by an outsider, though no married person ought to count himself or herself immune from such a temptation. The best protection here is to accept unquestionably the Church's viewpoint that marriage is for life. But other intrusions can spoil a marriage. A man's preoccupation with his work so that he never thinks of the outings from the house his wife requires. A woman's preoccupation with her family, so that she never thinks how her husband needs her interest in what he is doing. Surprisingly enough, relations can intrude between husband and wife, even children, and of course, the friends of one partner of whom the other disapproves. A marriage like an attractive garden needs to be guarded, and after the passage of years wisdom counsels that the fences be examined to see that they are still in repair.

Is it fanciful that I compare marriage to a garden? But the Bible draws a picture of our first parents in a garden, the garden of Eden, which is almost a synonym for paradise. To tarnish in any way that bright image of marriage would be my last wish, but if my words are to be true to the Bible, I must point out how the fall of man also took place in that garden, it took place through disobedience. So there are vows to be kept in marriage but they are designed for our ultimate happiness. Let us rejoice then today at God's priceless gift of love but let us, by means of that same grace of God do all in our power to protect it, or in the words of my text from 1 Timothy 6. 20, 'keep safe that which is entrusted to you.'

Home

> Deuteronomy 26. 9 *'He has brought us to this place and given us this land.'*

Uppermost in our minds today must be the thought that we have returned to the place from which we set out on a venture, because marriage is a venture and none of us quite knows how it will turn out. Deep down inside us we know this, and maybe one of the urges which has made us accept the invitation to attend this service is gratitude for the experience that our marriage has turned out well.

1 *Home*

Now there is one great difference for each couple here as compared with the wedding day about which every one of us is thinking, today we all have a home. A home is the first consequence of marriage. What each of you has built since you left this Church as husband and wife is a home, however simple, however grand. There is nothing better a woman can do for a man than to make him a home and only a woman can do it. A home gives a man the background of strength he cannot otherwise possess. He can of course relax in isolation after a fashion, he can relax in a different kind of way among his men friends; but only at home can he relax in company without having to strive, and where he is loved for being himself. Theodore Storm tells in an intriguing couplet how a man can endure all so long as his loved one lives:

> *So komme, was da kommen mag!*
> *So lang du lebest ist es Tag.*

A woman too needs a home, she needs it for her own self-fulfilment. She needs to make it herself around her, she needs a place to which to belong. When therefore men and women come together in their own homes there are scarcely any words too strong to describe its attractive power, its innate satisfaction and its enormous potential.

First of all then, each couple should thank God for the home they have been able to make, indeed, the factual statement of my text would serve for this purpose. 'He has brought us to this place and given us this land.' Please do not think I am forcing this text by letting 'land' stand for 'home.' Unless you are an Old Testament scholar you will probably not know the pull of this word 'land' in the Hebrew. It exercised the kind of extraordinary fascination that the word 'liberty' has done in our modern world. Simply to hear the word *eretz* still sends a thrill down the spine of an Israeli. To see the land (that is, Palestine), to plant a tree there, to pick up the soil and let it trickle through the fingers is to taste ecstacy. And the land means home. It is what God gave his people, a good land, a rich land, a land flowing with milk and honey, the complete contrast to the desert. No wonder Israel's poetry waxed lyrical over it and the book of Deuteronomy, from which my text is taken, could almost be described as a series of sermons about the land, Israel's home which God had provided. Once grasp this and the significance of my text stands out. 'He has brought us to this place and given us this land.' First of all today, then, thanksgiving to God that you have been given a home.

2 *Children*

Secondly, children. Every man or woman who has ever sat on a selection board sifting applicants for a job, every school teacher, every responsible employer will know the experience of spotting the candidate who comes from a good home. On the other hand, headmasters and headmistresses especially will tell with sorrow of the hardships under which boys and girls struggle who come from a broken home. There is no doubt that when they first arrive children give unwittingly to the home. They give to the parents. They give deep satisfaction, purpose for living and endless interest. These make the labours, the disturbed nights and the constant attention worth while. But the parents and the home they provide, give to the children more than they can forecast. Stability of background, understanding and significance are obvious, but there are many other gifts as well, some of which come not by direct imitation but by reaction. Wise husbands and wives will, therefore, give the priority in their home to their relationship to each other. If this is not right, very little they do for their children will be predictable. This is why our reunion service today is important, it brings husbands and wives back to each other as at the first, reminding how love is the basis of all that is good in the home. Then the children will be loved but not as overwhelming priorities, stifling them and hindering them from acquiring that independence of the home up to which they must in time grow.

'But the birth of a child is an uncontrollable glory;
Cat's cradle of hopes will hold no living baby.
  Long though it lay quietly.
And when our baby starts the struggle to be born
It compels humility. What we began
Is now its own.'

(Anne Ridler)

3 God's gift

Then there is the recognition of God. Throughout the book of
Deuteronomy there recurs a constant warning not to forget God
who gave the land and gave the home. To forget is easy when
success crowns our efforts and comforts multiply and our initial
struggles are memories of the past. Pride of achievement can so
easily replace gratitude for gifts, and when this takes place the
quality of the home suffers. It suffers because this way come tensions, divisions and at worst, break-up. 'A house' said Jesus,
'divided against itself cannot stand.' The best safeguard against
breakdown, which nobody wants, is unity on the part of husband
and wife and thankfulness to God for what he has given. And this
thankfulness must not only be inwardly felt but outwardly expressed. The Hebrew people were commanded to keep the
religious festivals. And festivals they were, with music and dancing. If this sermon is a serious affair it in no way precludes the
celebration of the anniversary of your wedding. Yes, with music
and dancing if such is your line. Great anxiety would indeed need
to be felt if you did not celebrate your wedding day with something out beyond the routine of your normal life. But remember
the religious part! It is God you must thank first, and at regular
intervals throughout your life. 'He has brought us to this place
and given us this land.' If you omit this, do not be surprised if for
the well being of your marriage anxiety is justified.

We have come together today in order to lift our married life
on to the highest level and to keep it there. As we look around we
see far too many instances of marriages that have not broken but
have simply become boring.

Louis Macniece, in a poem called *Les Sylphides* tells of a marriage
begun in the glamour of the ballet stage but which almost wholly
lost its glamour.

41

'So they were married—to be the more together—
And found they were never again so much together.
Divided by the morning tea,
By the evening paper,
By children and tradesmen's bills.'

Let us lift our marriage up by letting God come in. Let us thank him for our marriage and our home. Let us resolve to cultivate it in a spirit of thankfulness. And who will deny, certainly not the Bible, that in providing good homes in our nation today, beset with many troubles, more is being done for its well-being than all the institutions, laws and governments put together? In the last resort, the quality of a nation's homes makes it what it is.

II MOTHERS' SERVICE

Love and Wisdom

1 Peter 4. 8 *'Love covereth a multitude of sins.'*

Without a moment's delay this text calls for exposition lest it be taken wrongly. The word 'sin' according to its strict interpretation, means 'missing the mark.' It conjures up a picture of a man shooting arrows at a target, aiming of course for a bull's eye as every archer does, but missing it, perhaps missing the target altogether to everyone's amusement and his own disgust. Our text says love compensates for dozens of occasions when we fail to hit a bull's eye or indeed miss the target altogether. And that surely is a most arresting statement, not least when applied to the actions of a mother in the home. Love compensates for a host of occasions when we miss what we really hoped to achieve.

No mother is a perfect mother; a good mother, yes, but not a perfect mother. It is astonishing how many good mothers there are in the world. Middle-aged fathers not infrequently gaze at their daughters with amazement when they observe how competent as mothers, what they have counted as children, so quickly become. In a sense it is natural for a woman to become a good mother. But she is never perfect. She is never free from making mistakes, never immune from uttering some remark hurting to her child, or damaging his feelings by thoughtless action. More often than she knows she misses the mark. There never was, in fact, a perfect mother, the mother of Jesus being no exception, unless we subscribe to the doctrine of the Immaculate Conception. The wonder is that Jesus was what he was with the upbringing of a supremely good but imperfect mother.

1 *Love*

Love, however, compensates for a host of mistakes. Love is what a mother primarily provides, and if a child has never experienced a mother's love, God help him in later life! No love compares exactly with a mother's love. For one thing, it develops naturally. It could almost be asserted that a mother cannot help loving. We say that for a mother to neglect her children is unnatural. But a mother's love is more than mechanical, it is compounded with fascinated personal interest in her child's development, which never wholly leaves her. No interest endures like a mother's interest. Be her son a President, a Field Marshal, a farmer or an office worker, a mother, if she lives that long to see him arrive at this success, recognizing that he lives in a world cut off from hers, nevertheless never loses interest. What is more, the son, the daughter, is aware of the fact.

Two men were once sitting in a train at King's Cross, waiting for the guard's whistle. Suddenly a third man thrust himself into the compartment panting furiously. He had, as he burst out, 'just made it.' All at once he recognized one of the two fellow-passengers and broke in with some cheering remark. But the one addressed responded feebly. The newcomer, therefore, pressed on, talking excitedly about the Stock Exchange. Both men appeared as middle-aged and successful in their business. Then the half-silent man revealed self consciously that he had lost his mother. 'The funeral took place only last week', he said. But the information clearly fell on insensitive ears. Only one of those two had experienced the peculiar loss that is sensed when 'mother' dies, but when he did experience it the truth broke in that there is no love quite like a mother's, not even the love of a husband nor the love of a wife. A mother's love is compounded of interest for the object of her love alone and not in part, for herself.

As a mother you will make mistakes, that is certain, but if you

43

go on being yourself, if you go on loving, the mistakes will by this find in large measure their compensation. This is the ministry of love.

2 Wisdom

Secondly, there is in every mother an innate wisdom. Wisdom is not the same as cleverness and it is certainly not to be identified with book learning. Wisdom knows what fits with life, and this knowledge in a mother is partly intuitive, partly instinctive. She knows that there is a right way and a wrong way of doing things, and she knows too that the right way leads to happiness and the wrong way leads to unhappiness. She does not need this lesson to be drummed into her ears, she discovers it herself as the truth of life. Wise men will pay attention here because a mother has experienced and to some extent always retains, closer contact with fundamental existence than any other living creature. Men, even fathers, drift away into abstractions, mothers keep close to earth. It is not for nothing that we have the expression 'mother earth.' There is an innate earthy wisdom in her which belongs to the very nature of existence. A wise mother is in touch with truth.

3 Wise love

A mother's love and a mother's wisdom can however come into conflict. A mother can so possessively love her children that she smothers them. Wisdom counsels that if she is to retain their love she must foster their separation from herself. This is hard, yet in the long run it is the safeguard against the implication of what is commonly called 'the generation gap.' The mother of Jesus had to succumb to this hurting experience. In the Jerusalem temple, the boy Jesus, aged twelve, at the time of his Bar-Mitzvah, or confirmation, partly broke from his mother with the words, 'Don't you know that I must be about my father's business?' And later on, during his Galilean ministry, when she tried to interfere and bring him home, he separated himself from her claims with the remark that he who does God's will is his brother, sister and mother. But on the cross at the last, he did not forget her, he provided for her the home she needed in the house of his disciple, John, a tender man.

Love indeed makes up for a host of mistakes, but no mother, nor for that matter, anyone else, should trade on this—wisdom must counterbalance love, or the love that is offered will be rejected, and no pain is more painful than rejected love. Let love be paramount, therefore, and we shall be forgiven much, for we sin much, but let none of us fail to seek to apply that wisdom which involves restraint. So there will be fashioned, by God's grace, wise love, and wise love is the most creative attitude to people in all the world, the special attribute of all good mothers.

12   SCHOOLS SERVICE

Striving for the mastery

Philippians 4. 13 '*I have strength for anything through him who gives me power.*'

A short time ago a friend of mine was demonstrating his work on metal fatigue. He took a bar of steel twelve inches long, two inches wide and three-quarters of an inch thick. He inserted the ends of this bar into the jaws of a machine, pressed a button and the jaws slowly drew further and further apart, tearing that tough steel as if it were a piece of plasticine. Taking out the two pieces, he examined the fracture and set it on one side with similar broken bars of steel. Think of the strain on the fuselage of aircraft to sustain the force of propulsion through space! And it is only possible, as indeed all supersonic flight is only possible, because man is for ever wrestling to master his environment; in this case striving to produce substances sufficiently tough to resist enormous strains.

But all life, not only technological advancement, all life proceeds by way of mastering our environment.

A few days ago I watched a small boy learning how to walk. You know how it is. I didn't know whether to laugh or cry. First he struggled up on to his feet holding a chair. Then a few staggering steps followed by a flop. Tears nearly developed, but no, he was up again. Once more the staggering steps. Once more the collapse. But at last he mastered the technique. Next day of course he would do better and the day after better still. Einstein began in the same way, Winston Churchill, Beethoven, Dante and everyone else.

1 *Mastering our environment*

Life develops when people strive for the mastery of environment and of skills. Today there are thousands and thousands of new techniques waiting to be discovered. One important technique, I should have thought, would have been the desalinisation of sea-water at an economic price. Another would be the production of a battery sufficiently light to be incorporated in a car and so dispense with petrol and air pollution.

One of the key principles for living successfully is the mastery of environment. And it always proceeds by steps. I have described a baby learning to walk. Next there comes, perhaps, how to catch a ball, then maybe swimming, then climbing a rope, yes, and coming down again without tearing your hands! We cannot progress without mastering our environment.

2 Mastering situations

But I want to go on to something more difficult, mastering situations. Perhaps you will see what I mean if I tell you a story. It is about a boy aged fifteen and a girl slightly older. They were good friends. They enjoyed each others' company. But the boy cooled off. He wanted to excel at cricket and that takes time, and he wanted to do well in his examinations. In any case love never plays quite the same part in a boy's life as in a girl's. It is more on the surface, especially at first. So they stopped meeting. After a time the boy forgot the girl, but the girl did not forget him. Truth to tell, she really loved him. Not long after, she developed an incurable disease which wasted her pitifully. But she made a request. Could she see the boy again? Through the parents the meeting was arranged. He climbed the stairs and entered the bedroom. She was sitting up in bed waiting. He looked at her and was taken aback. Then he made a fatal mistake. He showed it in his face and, frightened, withdrew to the opposite corner of the room. Fumbling with his jacket button he made a remark about the weather, and the girl asked after his cricket. Little more was said and after a few minutes he withdrew stumbling into the street. In no way had he mastered that situation and he knew it. Shortly after the girl began that journey from which there is no return.

The whole community these last few years has made tremendous strides in mastering the environment, technological skills have surpassed themselves in their efficiency, but how little we have mastered human situations—Vietnam, Northern Ireland, employer and employee, the generation gap, the boy/girl relationships. We have not gained the mastery here, we are failing at every point.

I think what has impressed me most in my recent reading in the

New Testament is the astonishing mastery over human situations achieved by Jesus Christ. I have of course been familiar for a long time with the description of Jesus as Master in the sense of teacher, but what is also true is that he was always master of situations. A lunatic screamed out in a synagogue service; he was master there. A fisherman threw himself at Jesus' feet, embarrassingly laying bare his own private inadequacy; Jesus was master there. Radical theologians heckled in the market-place; he was master there. A whole hungry crowd in a desert place with no possibility of food could be ugly; but he was master there. A political trap all about taxation, purposely planted to make him appear hooked whichever way he answered; but he was master there. Even in the Praetorium before Pontius Pilate he mastered the situation and the procurator was discomfited. This is how I see Christ now, the supreme master of human situations. That is the kind of leader I need, and the community needs today. A master of situations, human situations.

3 *Mastery of self*

And now, mastery of ourselves. Not long ago I was enthralled by a superb presentation on television in *The Play of the Month* series, of *Girls in Uniform*. It was about a mistress under the appallingly strict discipline of a girls' school in East Prussia before the war. What captivated me was the astonishing mastery over her own emotions achieved by the assistant mistress doted on by some of the girls (and not surprisingly when you saw her). But this was where she showed her maturity over against their immaturity, she had mastered her emotions. They were there, but she mastered them.

A few minutes ago I told you about a boy who mishandled a situation badly with a diseased-wasted girl. Don't be too hard on him, he was only fifteen. But this is the point. It requires maturity to master ourselves. It really is childish to let our emotional life be spilled out all over the place for every one to see. Every one of us who is ever going to master a situation or an environment must first of all be master of self; master of feelings, master of instincts, master of appetites and master of emotions.

I believe the possibility of this mastery and this maturity is far greater for all who are ready to open their personalities to a power greater than themselves, and I believe that power is God known in Jesus Christ. It seems to me that what the gospels are crying aloud

47

to tell us is that Christ was the master because he was open to another level of being than the human. And it seems to me that what the Epistles in the New Testament are crying aloud to tell us is that we can be open to that same resource by means of commitment to Jesus Christ. Or as St Paul summarised it in a nutshell, 'I have strength for anything through him (Christ) who gives me power.'

All of us here are setting out to master life. It is a proper thing to do. My question is—with what are you going to achieve it? I have pointed to Jesus Christ, the supreme Master. I believe commitment to him to be the way of attaining mastery. 'I can do all things through Christ who strengthens me.' Philippians 4. 13 I can achieve the mastery.

13   PRIZEGIVING

The prize of life

1 Corinthians 9. 26 (N.E.B.) *'You know (do you not?) that at the sports all the runners run the race, though only one wins the prize.'*

I want to begin by asking if this is fair? All run so why do not all receive a prize? Equality of effort should mean equality of reward, or are you going to make excuses for the text by asserting that some runners did not try as hard? But will this hold? Is it not the case that at least some of those who brought up the rear engaged in as much training beforehand, if not more, than the one who breasted the tape first? To some athletes success comes easily. For one thing they may have been born with longer legs or more capacious lungs. No, a race is an unequal affair, all run but, only one (or perhaps two others, a 'silver' as well as a 'bronze'), receives a prize.

1 *Accepting the prize winners*
This, be it known, is a lesson we shall have to learn quickly in life or we shall go through it embittered. Only a select few receive the

obvious prizes and if this means an unfair inequality we shall have to put up with it. As a former Rector of the Imperial College of Science and Technology, London, used to say, 'There is nothing more unequal than an examination results list.' One is at the top, another is at the bottom and everyone else is somewhere in between. The only way to avoid this is to do away with all examinations and if this evokes a cheer, it is doubtful if we should be as happy to abolish athletics altogether; no more sports days! no more Olympic Games!

First, then, we must make up our minds, and that means most of us, to accept the situation without grudging that only a select few receive the prize.

2 Enter the contest to win

Secondly, we are advised to contend in the race, in the examination (for a race is a kind of examination), as if we were going to win, that is to say, we must not rule out the possibility of being 'placed' before we start. Every contestant has to put all he has into the contest. This is half the value of the contest, that it develops what each athlete has. In a way the race itself is the prize. Each athlete is the better for having stretched himself, better than the one who only watched from the grandstand. We may rightly deplore, therefore, the situation in one school where the boys had so worked out by computor who was bound to win that they cancelled the sports day fixture altogether. That way there was no prize for those whom the backroom boys had not 'placed.'

Two students were overheard talking on one of London's Underground stations on their way to sit their degree examination. 'Well,' said one to the other, 'I can't do more now, and even if I don't get my degree, I shall have the reward of having undergone the course.' And he was right. There is a reward for being in the race as well as for actually taking the prize.

3 Life's examination

Thirdly, let it be seen that examinations and prize giving do not end with school or university. Throughout life we are always sitting examinations. You will be examined by those with whom you work when you come to take up your first employment, or some new job after that. All your fellows will watch you day after day, testing for your weakness and testing for your strength. There is no principle of equality in the judgements (or examinations) of men. They are realists. You will be examined if ever you become a Managing Director and take the chair at your first board meeting. Each member of the board will watch, perhaps with hooded eyes, to note how you will handle your first knotty problem. You will be examined by thirty pairs of children's eyes if you become a school teacher, walking into your first classroom. 'What can we do with this teacher?' And every illness, every setback, every disappointment, yes, in love as well as in work (and this will happen), will constitute an examination. The question is not, shall we abolish examinations at school, but shall we pass the examinations that come after school?

4 Develop your gift

This leads on to a fourth point. There is a race in which all the contestants receive a prize at the start. They are, in fact, birthday presents or gifts. The New Testament uses a picture word and calls them 'talents.' Everyone is born with some talent. And the call is to exercise it. It could be physical prowess. It could be intellectual ability. It could be music appreciation. The call is to develop your distinctive gift in the economy of God. A community needs not only academic expertise or breathtaking acrobatics, but nurses, engineers, actors and hairdressers. Perfect the skill you possess and prize it, not because it exactly matches your neighbour's style, but because it is different. And this is the wisdom conveyed by the parable of the talents which Jesus told. Everyone who develops his skill is rewarded with the prize of developing added skill. Above all, seek the grace which Christ offers.

Let us then congratulate ungrudgingly those who have won prizes today, but let us remember that the prizes in the examinations of life go to those who recognize that examinations exist throughout life and that what is required is to commit ourselves to them, developing the gift we each one possess with the help of God.

Teaching with authority

Mark 1. 22 (N.E.B.) '*They were astounded at his teaching,
for, unlike the doctors of the law, he taught with a note of
authority.*'

This is the sharp point at which school teachers today feel that
they must leave Christ outside the classroom door. Teaching with
authority is 'out'. All pupils must be left to develop their own
potentiality free from indoctrination or imposed ideals. The whole
purpose of education is to encourage the young to develop their
own powers of reasoning and what they reason about is their own
affair. Education must be pupil-centred and subject-centred.

The question arises, however, is this view of education right or
is it half right? Is the contemporary repudiation of authority in
education due to a misinterpretation of what authority is or should
be? Has the teaching profession drawn its view of authority from
the repelling scenes of the Victorian classroom with its soulless
learning by rule and its ready use of the cane, which sordid conditions did not only obtain in the board schools but at Eton as well,
as graphically recorded by the Third Marquis of Salisbury in a
recent biography. So it would seem from a recent television programme which compared the work of Piaget and progressive
classrooms with representations of Dickens' Dotheboys Hall. Are
we not, therefore, suffering from polarization over this question
of authority in education? And is it not time that we took a hard
look at what authority properly understood really is? And is there
not a great deal to be said for looking at it in a service of worship
away from the politics which today dog the field of education at
every level, blurring the issues? Surely there is wisdom in reviewing
authority as Christ exemplified it! No one in his senses would
advocate a total repudiation of authority in education. It is by
authority that children go to school at all. The urgent question,
however, is—what is its nature? What can we learn from Christ of
whom it was reported in Capernaum that 'they were astounded
at his teaching, for, unlike the doctors of the law, he taught with
a note of authority.'

1 *Absence of sanctions*

First of all it is obvious, though too frequently overlooked that there were no sanctions. This was the overriding difference between Jesus as a teacher and the doctors of the law. He imposed no penalties, indeed, he had none he could impose. Fines, imprisonment and excommunication all belonged to the professionals and yet Jesus as a teacher wielded an authority which they lacked.

2 *Absence of coercion*

Secondly, it is clear that Jesus' authoritative way of teaching was accompanied by no coercion. Those who heard him were left to make their own decisions, indeed, they were encouraged to do so. A rich man was told to give away his riches but was left to depart without doing so. Cleansed lepers were ordered to report to the authorities, but Jesus made no effort to see that this was done. Even on the cross, when his fellow victim was suffering the pains of his own misdeeds, Jesus took no steps to advise him of the error of his ways, but left him alone to come to his own conclusions. 'Whas do you think?' 'What do you want?' These were the questiont which were frequently on the lips of this teacher. And yet he taught with authority!

3 *Personal trust*

Thirdly, we should notice that this teacher was crucified. That is to say, there arrived a time of ultimate confrontation, even so the teacher with authority did not overrule. We are able to see at this point, therefore, what is the real nature of breakdown, when it occurs, between the teacher and those to be taught. It is a breakdown of personal trust not a transgression of imposed rules.

All this enables us to discern what is the nature of a proper authority in the teacher, it is personal. The awareness of this in Jesus is what astounded the people of Capernaum when they first encountered him. And if we might be disposed to dismiss this as the amazement of an ignorant populace we ought also to note the assessment of Jesus by a Jew who was called 'the teacher of Israel', he affirmed how obvious it was that Jesus was a teacher come from God.

Can we not therefore see how the conflict is not between a teacher exercising authority by sanction and a lack of authority altogether? There is another kind of authority fearfully demanding on the teacher but which alone is proper to those who understand their teaching as a vocation, that is, as teachers 'come from God'. They do not tyrannize, they do not proselytize, they do not indoctrinate, they accompany their pupils on a voyage of intellectual discovery, but, and this is important, they believe that truth is given, not invented, and they have chosen to live by the things in which they believe. So values as well as techniques are involved in teaching, and above all there is a striving for the building up of personal relationships which is costly but without which no teaching can ultimately succeed.

Must Christ be left outside the door of the modern classroom? Will not disaster result for education if this is so? Christ as the teacher must be the teacher of teachers. And if the hard-worked, often underestimated and sometimes despised ranks of the teaching profession today, sometimes feel discouraged, let them remember this, that the greatest man of all time, the God-man, did not hesitate to be known as, and to bear, the honoured name of teacher.

15   YOUTH WEEK-END

Winning new strength

Isaiah 40. 30, 31
'Young men may grow weary and faint,
even in their prime they may stumble and fall;
but those who look to the Lord will win new strength,
they will grow wings like eagles;
they will run and not be weary,
they will march on and never grow faint!'

1 *The crescendo*

What an odd text this is! I don't mean the bit about growing wings like eagles. In fact I am going to alter it in line with the older version, 'they shall fly up with wings like eagles.' No, I mean it is an odd sort of crescendo. Here we are being told of a way new strength is won, and then, as an example, we have 'flying up with wings like eagles'; next, 'running and not being weary'; next, 'marching and never growing faint.' Flying, running, walking! What sort of crescendo is this? I should expect the next stage to be stopping still. If this is all 'looking to the Lord' can produce—a gradual slowing up process, then I couldn't blame anyone for having nothing to do with it!

But is it such an odd sort of crescendo after all? It is a kind of strength exhibition for a man to go leaping over a five-bar gate, or to sit up all night working on some project. But maybe many of us can achieve sudden spurts of energy and really surprise our friends. 'I never thought he had it in him,' but isn't it a far more severe test of a man's strength if he can not only accomplish sudden spurts but stick out the purpose he had in mind day after day, week after week, month after month till he has achieved his aim, without giving up? So perhaps this is a true crescendo after all—a man who wins new strength not only flies up as if on eagles' wings at some new challenge in his life, but goes on running tirelessly when the initial start is over, yes, and even continues marching on and on with no sign of growing faint, no sign of giving up. This indicates a remarkable reserve of strength, the strength of 'the sticker.'

2 Reserves

A reserve of strength is the great need. Here is a student faced with an examination. Is there really much value in sitting up late the night before working at the subject? He may spot the questions that will turn up. It must be admitted there is value in last minute revision, but everyone knows who has ever tackled an examination successfully that 'passes', and certainly 'honours', are only obtained by patient working at the subject months before the examination, building up a reserve of knowledge out of which to answer the questions.

Did you see on television an interview with a footballer belonging to one of the first-class teams who was summoned by the manager to his office because his play was insufficiently good and who was in consequence recommended to seek a transfer? He didn't enjoy this humiliating prospect but he was no fool. It was the end of the season and he set himself during the intervening months before the next season to put his defects right, not least to increase his speed. And it worked. The steady training paid off. He so increased the quality of his play that all talk of transfer next season, when it came, was completely dropped.

Here is a girl in a choral society in the north of England with an unusual timbre to her voice. Her father who sang bass brought her along but rated her chances very low of being much more than one extra voice. But she took singing lessons to develop the gift she felt she possessed, and now she is a soloist with considerable prospects.

Success in any walk of life depends on the patient, plodding work behind the scenes building up resources of knowledge, skill and expertise so that when the testing time arrives, the issue is almost certain.

3 The compass

Success, however, in life does not only depend on knowledge and skill, it depends on temperament and character. Perhaps this is seen nowhere more clearly than in the finals of the women's singles at Wimbledon. Almost everything depends there on not cracking under the strain and the publicity.

Now there is much more to life than passing a public examination, singing a solo or acquiring professional status in some sport. To begin with the testing time is longer and the consequences more lasting. We need spiritual resources for successful living, by which I mean living that does not flag, become embittered and appear as a mere long endurance test. And these spiritual resources are found by 'looking to the Lord'—to quote the words of my text. But what does this mean? Let me give you an illustration.

Here is a man, or it could be a woman, for women have attempted it—sailing solo across the Atlantic. There is one necessity to be carried out every morning and every evening whatever the weather conditions and whatever the conditions of health of the navigator—and that is to check the position of the ship by the compass.

Here then is the wise precaution which everyone who wishes to succeed takes throughout the voyage of his life. Every now and again, certainly once a day, he checks his position by reference to Christ. Has his conduct been in line with what Christ would approve? Are his aims in conformity with what Christ would label as honest? Does he really care about anyone else or are his sights only set upon himself? Christ is the proper compass for living to which everyone should refer. And whoever does so makes this discovery—he wins new strength, exhibiting it in a true crescendo as my text from Isaiah Chapter 40 expresses it:

'Young men may grow weary and faint,
even in their prime they may stumble and fall;
but those who look to the Lord will win new strength,
they will grow wings like eagles;
they will run and not be weary,
they will march on and never grow faint.'

Where Christianity Offends

A friend of mine lives in London close to the Albert Hall. Once a week, on his day off, he motors through South London on his way out to the country past a two-storied detached house which, believe it or not, has stood half finished for twenty years until last year, when it was suddenly completed and occupied. Of course he has wondered why. Couldn't the builders get the drains right? Did the owner lose interest in the structure? Did they reckon it too ultra-modern for the late 1940s—or did the cash simply run out?

Jesus once told a story of a man who set out to build a tower but left it half-finished because he hadn't the wherewithal to complete it. He said people mock at that kind of half-sighted individual; and he capped it with a story of a military campaigner who failed to make a reckoning beforehand whether or not he possessed sufficient strength to overcome his adversary. The point of both stories is that any would-be follower of Christ must count the cost of discipleship before committing himself, otherwise he is going to look very silly. So the title for my sermon is 'Where Christianity offends.'

Let me begin with a differentiation. There are points in the Christian faith which offend but which can be cleared with a little explanation. But there are others which explanation only makes more offensive. I want to deal with both these kinds.

First, the kind of offence which a little explanation clears up. For example, the exclusive claims of Christianity—'I am the way, the truth and the life.' But what about Hinduism? What about Buddhism? What about Islam? Is there no truth in them? No way to God at all? No spiritual awareness in consequence?—Then how have they persisted down the centuries? And how have they won the allegiance of millions? Is not this exclusive claim of Christianity offensive, offensive to the intellect?

And my answer is—we do not assert that there is no pathway to God, no truth, no life in these other faiths—what we declare is that the way, the truth and the life have been uniquely focussed in Jesus Christ. He is like a burning glass by means of which the diffused rays of the sun are concentrated at one point with effective results. Because Christ is the light the implication is not that all else is dark but that 'in his light we can see light, and in his straight path we may not stumble.'

The apparently exclusive claim of Christ is an example of the kind of offence that may be cleared up with further elucidation.

But what of the second kind of offences which no explanation will remove? Let me give three examples and the first is the particularity of the Christian message. This is what I mean. If the Christian gospel were couched simply in terms of general truths of reason, offering a philosophy of existence and a code of ethics following therefrom—who would object? But it puts forward instead a man who lived, or is said to have lived, in Palestine at the time of the Roman occupation, who had to be taught the elements of personal hygiene like the rest of us, who spoke a dialect of Hebrew, who never wrote any books and whose utterances therefore as well as his very existence are all subject to the vicissitudes of historical enquiry. And did Christ teach timeless truth? If not, why set him up so high? And if he did how can they be particularised in one man and that man the product of the first century? So God become flesh, the Christian doctrine of the Incarnation, is an offence and we cannot get round it.

Secondly, the Cross of Christ is an offence. Of course we have tried to get round this. All the world's topmost artists and sculptors have presented it as an artistic masterpiece, and how wonderfully they have succeeded. But the crucifixion of Jesus was not a thing of glory. How the Jews, who loathed nudity, ever got round to accepting a man strung up naked on a stake of wood in public can only be understood by seeing it as a sign of the extent to which their hate had run. Of course we have known for a long time what a crucifixion was like but since 1968 and the discovery of some cave tombs north of Jerusalem we now have the evidence of the remains of a crucified man called Jehohanan. Apparently Jesus' forearms were pierced and not his hands and one leg was wrapped over the other so that the crutch could rest on the *sedecula*. The feet were fastened one on top of the other with one nail. Then the zig-zag contorted victim could last in torture for days. Of course we have glamorised the crucifixion. Could you expect us to tell of the flies, the screaming, the performance of the bodies' natural functions in public, the stench. Yet this is Christianity's chief symbol. There are dignified, even impressive ways of dying; Socrates, for example, drinking the hemlock while he discoursed with his friends. But crucifixion is lewd, revolting and an offence to every canon of decent taste. And even if we cover our eyes from the exhibit itself, the implication is ghastly—when a good man did nothing but good to his fellows, 'the man for others', this was his reward from them. What does the Cross show but the rottenness of the common, human heart of man? We find the Cross, I say, a thing of irremovable offence.

And who among us will say as Peter did the night before it took place, 'Though all shall be offended, yet will not I', and will not hear the re-echoing words of Christ himself, 'Before the cock crow twice, thou shalt deny me thrice.' The whole thing is an offence.

Third, the Christian Church; it is part of the gospel and it is an offence. 'I could accept Jesus Christ,' cried Nietzsche, or words to that effect, 'did he not come with his leprous bride the Church.' And all the 'Jesus kids' who have never heard of Nietzsche, say 'Amen!' And who is this unpopular theologian St Paul, writing to the Ephesians, 'Christ loved the Church and gave himself for it.' All this stuff about the Church being the bride of Christ. What is the game? To stream off business for Church-men? 'You can't have Christ without us'. . . . And is there not truth enough in that barb to bring blood? The Church has at all times sought to imprison Christ behind ecclesiastical walls. . . . For all that, the Church *is* part of the gospel. Jesus scarcely began to preach in Galilee before he had chosen his disciples. This is the offence—Christ does not come alone. He comes with his disciples and we have to live with his disciples if we would live with Christ.

The Incarnation, the Cross, the Church, these are the points where Christianity offends and we shall be fools to try to build our tower of Christian faith without recognizing at the outset that these are some of the expensive stumbling blocks of masonry we shall have to try to cement into the structure.

What more can I say? If I cannot explain away these offences shall I apologise for them? I don't think so. Indeed, I can't because I am not responsible. I, too, bear their offence. But there is St Paul who said that the foolishness of God is wiser than men, and I go on wondering if anything has touched mankind so deeply and extensively as the points of offence I have listed—the Christ child in the manger, the sufferer on the Cross bearing our pain, the mediocre Church, the fellowship of mediocre Christians.

Yes, Christianity is an expensive item and the cost is rising. So we had better think twice before we embark on it—though expensive things are valuable.

Let me end with a text since I did not begin with one. Luke 14. 28, 29. 'For which of you, intending to build a tower, sitteth not

down first, and counteth the cost, whether he have sufficient to
finish it? Lest haply, after he hath laid the foundation, and is not
able to finish it, all that behold it begin to mock . . .'

17 HOSPITAL WARD SERVICE

The patient's contribution

Luke 18. 41 (N.E.B.) '*What do you want me to do for you?*'
"*Sir, I want my sight back,*" *he answered.*'

Here is a conversation that took place on a dusty road in a hot
country, and it is worth our while giving it some attention because
of what it has to tell us about recovering from an illness. An illness
is like falling into a ditch. It is never planned. It happens quite
suddenly and almost always unexpectedly. But the getting out
process is much more difficult. It takes time and it takes thought,
and when on the bank once more, attention needs to be given to
cleaning up. There is an old Dutch proverb which says, 'Illness
comes on horseback and goes away on foot.'

Our conversation piece, however, and the short story from
which it is taken, has much more to give us than good advice of a
psychological kind. It places the whole situation of the doctor and
patient in the context of the presence of God which is all about us
and of which we are so often so little conscious, but which is concerned for our wholeness.

This story concerns a blind man sitting by the road-side begging.
Defective eyesight is much more common in hot countries than
in cooler climates, partly because children's eyes are not always
adequately protected against flies. This man in our story could be
one such. He had heard, however, of people recovering their
sight, and he had heard of the name of Jesus of Nazareth in this
connection. So when the day came and his sharp ears informed
him that an unusually large crowd was shuffling along the road, he
enquired what was happening, and when the reply was given that
Jesus of Nazareth was passing by, no remonstrations on the part of
the crowd were sufficiently severe to suppress his insistent *eleison*,

'Son of David, have pity on me.' And when Jesus stopped and magisterially summoned the man to be brought, he did not at once heal him. Instead he enquired, 'What do you want me to do for you?' as if his need were not already plain. But the asking was important for the healing, and the answer was important for the healing. And when the blind man replied unhesitatingly and submissively, 'Sir, I want my sight back', Jesus said, 'Have back your sight; your faith has cured you.'

Now this story, like all the stories in the gospels, has a meaning at various levels. Our concern, however, must be with the whole process of recovery from illness or getting out of the ditch into which we have unfortunately fallen.

1 The will and recovery

First, the story tells us that in illness there must exist the will to recovery. My mind goes back to a night during the war when the flying bombs were raining down on London. A young man was taken with sudden abdominal pains which the doctor diagnosed as calling for instant surgery. And as he lay on a stretcher on the pavement waiting to be lifted into an ambulance, his wife, who knew that his experience of illness was minimal, gave him this good advice in the form of a question. 'You will fight for it, won't you?' And the fighting became necessary because a lung collapsed when the surgeon finished and days followed with the oxygen cylinder. The nurses fought for his life but so did the patient, remembering in his semi-consciousness his wife's insistent question, 'You will fight for it, won't you?' So he crawled back to health and strength.

This is the point, the first necessity in illness is to exercise strongly the will to be well. This is what the blind man magnificently exemplifies in our story. Hearing a crowd he cocked his ear, enquired the meaning, cried out his plea, 'Son of David, have pity on me'. And when asked, 'What do you want me to do for you?' came up with a firm, clear, pressing request, 'Sir, I want my sight back.' The doctors, the nurses, the radiographers and all the rest can do little for us if we have not the will to be well.

2 Submission

Secondly, the patient has to submit. Submission is implied in the very word 'patient'. He has to suffer things done to him. He has to suffer first of all what the incidence of the illness has done to him.

60

Rebellion, revolt and militancy are all the fashion at the moment, but they existed long before on beds of sickness, and this is a place where they never win. There is absolutely no good to be derived from resenting what has happened. Fretting, asking 'why?' and being angry with God, our luck or life in general get an ill man nowhere at all. The right attitude for him if he wishes to be well, is to take what has come, to accept it and abandon all bitterness. 'It is no use crying over spilt milk'. The only profitable action is to set about acquiring some more.

So submit to the doctors, submit to the nurses, submit to the indignities. It is the only road to recovery. This blind man did not complain to Jesus, he called him 'Sir' which implies submission. It is the proper place from which to begin the climb to health and strength.

3 Faith

Thirdly, you will notice how the word 'faith' comes into the story. Let me repeat the last part of the conversation between the blind man and Jesus. 'Have back your sight', he said, 'your faith has cured you.'

In the last few years there has been a growing awareness of the part played by the mind upon the body. It really is old-fashioned now to conceive of the body as a kind of machine which can be tinkered with quite apart from what the patient thinks or believes. What a man thinks, what a man believes, has considerable effect on how his body functions. People full of fears are very slow to recover, if ever they wholly do. Faith, however, is the antidote to fear, and healing is very slow to come till the fears are banished.

At the very lowest level, to believe that it is possible to be well is essential. It is essential too to believe in the doctors and nurses, that is to say, to trust them. But more than either, it is necessary to believe that they are actually accomplishing God's healing purpose for mankind which is accomplished when the patient co-operates. This blind man in our story co-operated. Sightless though he was, he made his way to the healing Christ, putting himself in the position for healing and accepting what was offered.

Is there anything to be gained from illness and from a spell in hospital? Yes, there is. As one writer has expressed it, 'Sickness sensitizes man for observation like a photographic plate.' You will see more of the inner meaning of life after what you have experienced within these walls. And as André Gide, who was not a

Churchman, wrote, 'Those who have never been ill are incapable of real sympathy for a great many misfortunes.'

So the sick man should respond positively to his sickness and he will be the better person for all that he has suffered, for the fact of God's universal presence is the truth of life, and God is not indifferent to what we need.

18   NURSES' SERVICE

Four determined nurses

> Mark 2. 3, 4 (N.E.B.) '*And while he was proclaiming the message to them, a man was brought who was paralysed. Four men were carrying him, but because of the crowd they could not get him near. So they opened up the roof over the place where Jesus was, and when they had broken through they lowered the stretcher on which the paralysed man was lying.*'

I would like to bring to your attention today four male nurses. Perhaps you have never thought of them as nurses, not because they weren't women (and we usually think of nurses as female, though less so in our modern world), but because they are not specifically labelled as nurses in the story where their existence is recorded. Nevertheless they performed the service which belongs to nurses, they brought an ill man to the place of healing. The four nurses to whom I refer are the four men who carried a case of paralysis and set him down before Christ, indeed, so determined were they to bring their patient to what they believed to be a source of wholeness that they refused to be barred from access by a crowd and broke up the roof, letting down the sick man on a stretcher to the place where Jesus was standing. Here then were four determined nurses, determined to stop at nothing to place their patient in the way of recovery.

1 *What does nursing require?*

(a) Nursing requires first a firm conviction as to where healing can be found. This relates to the medical treatment which is being undertaken, to the physician or surgeon engaged in the case, and (let us not forget) to God himself who is the source of all healing. (See Exodus 15. 26.)

(b) Nursing also requires determination. After all, an ill person is (temporarily) weakened. He cannot always make up his mind, especially if the treatment required is unpleasant or painful or inconvenient. The nurse must will for him. He/she says what is to be done. The nurse takes charge. This is what the four men did who brought the paralytic to Christ.

(c) But nursing also needs the exercise of compassion. Firm conviction and determination without compassion can be formidable. They are insufficient by themselves. They need balancing. Similarly, compassion by itself is an inadequate qualification for a nurse. It is possible to be so sorry for the patient that the nurse never gets him to go through with the treatment.

2 What is the purpose of healing?

To bring the patient to the position of:

(a) Health, that is, wholeness of body, mind and spirit.
(b) Strength, that is, in order to accomplish what he will.
(c) Independence. No one is cured until he can stand on his own feet. The nurse and the patient must come to the point of independence of each other.

3 Who is the healer?

The doctor, the nurse, the environment, yes, and the patient, but there is no complete recovery without God, the source of wholeness. The greatest task of nursing is to bring those in need into the presence of God whom we encounter supremely in the person of Jesus Christ. This action may require words, it may not require words. We are not told that the four male nurses who carried their paralytic patient on a stretcher preached to him. But theirs was a Christ-like ministry.

So I want to leave you thinking about the bearing of your nursing ministry. Is it Christ-like? In coming into contact with your ministry do your patients come into contact with something Christ-like? If so, the influence is incalculable.

The winds of renewal

John 3. 4 (N.E.B.) ' *"But how is it possible"*, *said Nicodemus*, *"for a man to be born when he is old?"* '

Proof is impossible but probability is not ruled out that Nicodemus was old when he asked this question. 'With the ancient is wisdom' says the book of Job, 'and in length of days understanding.' So we may guess that the 'teacher of Israel' in Jesus' time, the man to whom everyone listened, was grey-headed. *Zaqen* was the word the Hebrews used both for an old man and a ruler or elder of the city and it occurs frequently in the Old Testament. Nicodemus then, we may suppose, was old, bearded and what the book of Ezra calls *Sab*, that is, grey-headed. So we see him in the fourth gospel in conversation with Jesus, a young man, at least a man about thirty.

It appears as if Nicodemus' visit was a surprise one. We are told that it was carried out under cover of darkness. That Nicodemus should visit Jesus at all is remarkable. Nicodemus was one of the top people in Jerusalem, living no doubt in a substantial and well-appointed house. He belonged to one of the aristocratic families which later on may have supplied Aristobulus with his ambassador to Pompey, and may even have negotiated the surrender terms of Jerusalem to the Romans. Do not, therefore, underrate Nicodemus, he was no ordinary Scribe or Rabbi. Indeed, he is not called such in the New Testament, but an *Archon*, or ruler of the Jews. It would not be difficult to visualize this man summoning the carpenter of Nazareth to his chambers for questioning. What we see, however, is the reverse. We see Nicodemus visiting Jesus' humble lodging and that under cover of darkness. I say the incident is remarkable.

Under these circumstances we may be sure that Nicodemus was prompted by more than curiosity. He had searching questions to ask about life's problems. But scarcely had the characteristic diplomatic overture crossed his lips than he found himself framing his incredulous question—'But is it possible for a man to be born when he is old?' Is it not true that when a man is old he is set, no power on earth can alter this situation.

As we turn this over in our minds, may we not suppose that Nicodemus was talking out of experience? Had he perhaps arrived at the day when he could read the small script on his parchments no longer? Was there some pain in his limbs with which at last he had to come to terms, for all the remedies he had tried had proved powerless to disperse it? Was he compelled perhaps to take his time over that walk to Jesus' lodging, for at his age he quickly ran out of breath? It seems unlikely that he was at the stage, as one writer puts it, when 'all a man's contemporaries are his friends', for in that case he would scarcely be out at night. No, Nicodemus had entered the autumn of life, and autumn has its attractions, or John Donne could never have written:

> 'No spring, no summer beauty hath such grace
> As I have seen in one Autumnal face.'

Nicodemus, I think, was attractive, he had never 'given up' as we say, but rather belonged to that group which Aeschylus alludes to in his Agamemnon:

'Old men who are always young enough to learn with profit.'
So he sets out at night to ask questions, questions of Jesus, and if we are wise we shall do the same, and especially to ask this one: 'Is it possible for a man to be born when he is old?'

The flesh and the Spirit

If we listen carefully to these two deep in conversation that night in Jerusalem with the wind blowing in gusts along the streets outside we shall notice how their scales of reference are diametrically opposed. Nicodemus limits everything by the flesh, Jesus limits everything by the Spirit. And because Nicodemus limits everything by the flesh, that is, by the material, everything is conditioned, everything is predictable. In the case of the body the arteries will harden, the pulse slow down, the eyes grow dim and the muscles weaken. The seven ages of man were well understood in Nicodemus' day and it was possible to calculate in general terms how each decade of life would be experienced.

> 'The days of our age are threescore years and ten, and though men be so strong that they come to fourscore years: yet is their strength then but labour and sorrow, so soon passeth it away and we are gone.'

Thus the Psalmist. And the man who sees no more than this is likely to settle down with the depressing words of Ovid the Latin poet—'When the roses are gone, nothing is left but the thorns.'

Jesus, however, was not depressing because he did not find the focus of life in the flesh which decays but in the Spirit which is deathless. And the Spirit is for ever creating unexpected patterns, fresh possibilities, even new life. In the Bible the word for Spirit is the same as for wind. *Ruach* in the Hebrew, *Pneuma* in the Greek. And God was constantly employing the wind to bring about new situations; at the Red Sea in the book of Exodus, at the Jordan river in the book of Joshua, in the valley of dry bones in the book of Ezekiel, and before the city of Nineveh in the book of Jonah. All this is summed up nowhere so neatly as in Psalm 147, 'He bloweth with his wind and the waters flow', crying aloud this one insistent, buoyant message that God, by his Spirit can change the most unpromising conditions into places of significance.

All this the young man Jesus brought home powerfully to the old man Nicodemus when suddenly he said, 'Listen to the wind, Nicodemus, thou hearest the sound thereof, but canst not tell whence it cometh or whither it goeth. So is every one that is born of the Spirit.'

It is true, of course, that this scripture is of wider application than to the restrictions of life when we grow older, but it does apply there too. New horizons, new attitudes, new graces, new features of character are possible in later life so transforming of personality from the general run that only the words 'new birth' will suffice.

It is very tempting when talking about the latter span of life to dwell on the compensations for losing one's youth, and they do exist. Someone has said, 'There are more pleasures on the other side of baldness than young men even think possible.' We might make a list. The old dare to be more independent, they take setbacks in their stride, they are more philosophical. And if some pleasures lose their tang, so does the bite of some temptations. But all this talk of the compensations of old age, satisfactory no doubt, as far as it goes, does not come near the offer of the Christian gospel which is that new life can be born by the power of the Spirit, evidenced by a radiance and concern for new things, young people and their troubles, not normally characteristic.

Death as birth

Of course the day of our departure will come. The life in the Spirit for all its transforming power does not cancel out the inherent nature of the flesh which is to pass away. But for the Christian even the death-day is the birthday which is why in our Church's calendar we commemorate the saints on their death-days and not on their birthdays. The day of their departure, as with all of us, is the day of rebirth into that fulness of life and 'those unspeakable joys which God has prepared for those that unfeignedly love him.' Some people have so grasped this viewpoint that they have looked forward to death with excitement, among whom was the late Lord Fisher, Archbishop of Canterbury, who said he could scarcely wait to discover the answers on the other side to the many questions which had puzzled him on this.

So we come back to Nicodemus' question—Is it possible for a man to be born when he is old? The majority will answer 'No', if they do not count the question too ridiculous for serious attention. But Jesus answers, 'Yes, it is.' It is possible by opening out the life to the Spirit of God, to be rid of the inward-looking attitude, the fretfulness, impatience with the young, hatred of everything new, the complaint of being unwanted—all this can be blown away by the winds of God and their place taken by buoyancy and expectancy. All clergymen have encountered examples of this in their ministry, indeed, it is what the Christian gospel is all about, or as St Paul expressed it—'No wonder we do not lose heart. Though our outward humanity is in decay, yet day by day we are inwardly renewed. . . . Meanwhile our eyes are fixed, not on the things that are seen, but on the things that are unseen, for what is seen passes away, what is unseen is eternal.'

20   A FUNERAL

A handrail

> 1 Thessalonians 4. 13, 14 (N.E.B.) *'We want you not to remain in ignorance, brothers, about those who sleep in death; you should not grieve like the rest of men, who have no hope. We believe that Jesus died and rose again; and so it will be for those who died as Christians; God will bring them to life with Jesus.'*

These are strong words, making a handrail on which to hold; and at a time like this, as in some fierce storm when thick black clouds obscure the sunshine, if not the light itself, and the winds bend almost to breaking point even the stoutest trees, nothing is more important than something strong on which to hold. What do these words say?

1 Death is a sleep

They say—and we ought to remember that what we have here is an extract from one of St Paul's letters to some of his earliest converts, men and women who were beginners, so to speak, in the Christian faith, and who were beaten down with the bereavements that had overtaken them—Paul's words say first of all, 'We want you not to remain in ignorance, brothers, about those who sleep in death.' Ignorance was what Paul strove to dispel because ignorance can be the root cause of paralysing fear. Have we not at some time seen parents pull aside the curtains in a child's bedroom to convince him that his fears are groundless?—There is no face peering through the glass! Paul, by his very use of the word 'sleep' to describe death disabuses us at one stroke of every idea of the finality of death. Sleep is an experience from which we shall awake. That is how it will be with death. The Bible would not have us struggle on in ignorance of this basic truth.

2 Hopeful grief

Secondly, Paul's words urge us not to grieve like the rest of men who have no hope. Grieve, of course, we shall, and grieve we must. Did not even our Lord himself shed tears at the grave of his friend Lazarus? Followers of Christ are not called to be stoics forcing themselves to display no kind of emotion, for this is inhuman, and Christ was never that. But we are bidden not to grieve like the rest of men who have no hope. There is a world of difference between hopeless grief and hopeful grief. It is the latter which should characterise Christians in their bereavement. 'Hard pressed on every side,' wrote Paul in another letter, 'we are never harrassed or bewildered, we are never at our wits' end; hunted, we are never abandoned to our fate; struck down, we are not left to die.' And the difference is made entirely by the hope we have that death is at most a sleep; it is not the end.

3 The historical basis

Thirdly, Paul comes down firmly on the ground of our hope—'We believe that Jesus died and rose again.' There is an historical basis for our faith. Jesus lived and Jesus died, yes, as far as anything historical can be proved, so can Jesus' life and death. And if we cannot go on to prove that Jesus rose again, to disprove it is equally difficult. Our faith in the resurrection of Jesus, therefore, is not without reason. It cannot be dismissed as mere wishful thinking. There are grounds for our belief. We are not crossing a swamp on which there is no firm foothold. This is why Paul can continue with his strong assertion for the Christians in Thessalonica and for us as well—'and so it will be for those who died as Christians; God will bring them to life with Jesus.'

I know of course that today's path is exceedingly rough. I can sympathise that you are wondering how you can possibly go on. But you will go on. Others have gone on. And there is this handrail which makes all the difference. 'God will bring them to life with Jesus.' And if I understand the providence of God at all, help will come to you now, meeting your present need in unexpected ways. God does not forget us.

21   SOCIAL WORKERS' SERVICE

The personal factor

John 5. 6 (N.E.B.) '*When Jesus saw him lying there and was aware that he had been ill a long time, he asked him, "Do you want to recover?"* '

This man had been a cripple for thirty-eight years. Whether or not it was for thirty-eight years that some one had carried him to the pool of Bethesda hoping for healing by its supposed curative waters, we are not told, but this is the impression given by the account. So the picture is one of entrenched impoverishment of life. To this man human existence brought only incapacity, almost total dependence on others and the cramping daily sight of little else but a narrow pool of water with maimed, deformed and aching limbs creaking to lower themselves into it (if they were able, and this one was not), believing that when the spring bubbled, deliverance would be granted to their ailing bodies.

There are some conditions of life which make the heart ache for their debilitating restrictions. Life simply goes round and round like a wheel with nothing more than the routine of a sick room, the unequal struggle to give some sordid dwelling the semblance of a home, the eking out of a pitiable pension in the loneliness of advancing old age. This is the pattern too often social workers see a drabness hidden from the brashness of contemporary affluence.

Meine Ruh' ist him
Mein Herz ist schwer
Ich finde sie nimmer
Und nimmermehr

So wrote Goethe of the girl at her spinning wheel.

My peace is gone,
My heart is heavy.
I shall never find it.
No, never, never.'

There is a hurting poignancy about this debilitating drabness couched in the awareness that much of it need never be. Callous unconcern on the part of the comfortable has all too often suffered the existence of those appalling conditions with a shrug of the shoulders. 'If you help these people they only relapse into their own slough.' There is enough truth in this assertion to account for its survival. There is a form of assistance which can be supplied that does not work for the sufferer's wholeness. What that assistance needs to be ought surely to concern the close attention of every social worker anxious to justify his labour.

1 *The sufferer's co-operation*

So we return to the text and the incident in which it is set. 'When Jesus saw him lying there and was aware that he had been ill for a long time, he asked him, "Do you want to recover?" '

Healing does not come in any lasting way to the unfortunate whose co-operation is not enlisted in the healing process. Unless an impoverished man's imagination is fired, his mind is alerted and his will stiffened, so that he stands on his own feet, though he be patched up, he will return again to his benefactors for assistance yet more and even more. Welfare that profits is not the mere improvement of the environment, the performance of an operation on the body as if it were a car gone wrong, or the provision of cash, all these ministrations are too external to be lasting. Everything depends on what the deprived wants. 'Do you want to recover?' That is what Jesus asked the cripple. It was not a stupid question.

Please note that the question was asked. Jesus did not retreat with the excuse, 'Thirty-eight years at the pool? What is the use of asking him?' On the surface this was indeed a hopeless case. But Jesus had more hope of the apparently hopeless than some of the outwardly comfortable apparently possess. He addressed this man (I did not say this 'case'), and he responded eagerly, rose to his feet cured, and did not return for treatment he had come to cherish. It was health he wanted, not medicine. And until a sufferer reaches such a state of mind he cannot enjoy recovery.

2 The personal is demanding

Social work at this level is however demanding of time and demanding of personal resources. There is not one of us who has supplied the beggar with a ready coin when he has intruded on our time without feeling afterwards that we have acted cowardly, having accomplished very little good. But have we the time? Have we the personal resources? These are the hard questions for every social worker. If we do not believe that people are pawns in a political game to be pushed around, or cogs in a social machine merely to be turned, we shall not seek to help, whatever kind or level of help is required, without involving our persons in the helping act. When Jesus healed the woman with the haemorrhage he felt that strength had gone out of him. Assistance towards health requires not only the movement of the heart of the afflicted towards the healer but also the movement of the heart (as well as the skill) of the healer towards the afflicted. Only when this two-way personal involvement is engaged is there healing after the pattern of Christ's work, but Christ himself is actually at work where this pattern is being followed even though the participants be unaware of it.

3 The source of healing

Note that Jesus addressed the cripple first. His was the source of recovery which the deprived lacked. Personal resource is what every healer, every social worker who achieves personal good requires. Part of the healing is in the healer, at least he is the personal mediator of the healing. It cannot be conveyed by mechanisms. This greatest recognition of the indispensibility of the personal element is what perhaps is needed more than ever in our contemporary, concrete, mechanical and computor age. We persons who are healers, healers of diseases, healers of social maladjustments, healers of all kinds of crippled relationships and situations, what more important requirement than that our person should be enriched by a deepening mystical experience with the person of Christ himself. Let the divine-human Christ touch our human and potentially divine labours with the power of his Spirit and who knows what transformations we shall by his grace be chosen to accomplish.

22 PUBLIC SERVANTS' SERVICE

Compromise and pardon

> 2 Kings 5. 18, 19 ' "When I bow myself in the house of Rimmon: the Lord pardon they servant in this thing." And he said unto him, "Go in peace." '

And we are astonished, perhaps even offended. So much so that we go to the lengths of drawing down the blinds over this scripture. Surely something must be wrong! Or can we perhaps discover some subtle exposition able to explain away what we do not wish to hear?

But you ask, what is the trouble? What is the difficulty over this scripture? The difficulty is that General Naaman, the *persona dramatis*, was converted from idolatry to faith in the living God, but when he was about to return to Syria where Rimmon was worshipped, he asked for pardon to worship him also, because his job required it.

1 *Compromise*

Here then is a man who understands clearly at the time of his conversion what he ought not to do, but he has no intention of abandoning it. He will go on believing, but he will go on misbehaving. This is the moral problem of this scripture. General

Naaman appears as a hypocrite, a coward, a man more concerned with convenience than with truth.

And as if this were not sufficient in itself to bewilder, General Naaman asks for pardon for his wrong doing before he commits it. That is to say, he not only fails to repent of his sin but actually asks for forgiveness knowing that he intends to commit it. Can there be any sincerity in such a man as this?

Even so, we have not plumbed the depths of the awkwardness of this scripture, and for this reason, that if we attempt to excuse Naaman as a new convert to his new faith, and therefore as yet insensitive and unspiritual, we are faced with the problem of Elisha, the man of God, from whom Naaman asked the forgiveness, bidding him, 'Go in peace.' And it was no 'hole-in-the-corner' forgiveness. Elisha came out to meet General Naaman and his military entourage which was more than he did when Naaman first presented himself at Elisha's door with a request for healing from his leprosy. On that occasion Elisha merely replied through the mouth of his servant—'Go, wash in Jordan seven times.' And the General was furious at such offhandedness. What military 'top-brass' wouldn't be! But Elisha, a prophet of the living God, was not going to be treated as some cheap oriental witch-doctor. So he acted imperiously. When, however, the General returned from the Jordan river, humbled and healed, Elisha met him in person, and promised forgiveness for the sin he intended to commit in advance. That is the problem.

One more point before we consider the implications when General Naaman met Elisha, he made three requests, the first of which was refused. This was that Elisha should receive payment for the cure of his leprosy. But he would take nothing. The second request was that he, Naaman, might transport back to Syria a small quantity of Israelitish soil on which to stand and worship the God of Israel. Superstition? But the request was granted. Thirdly, timidly we may guess because he both preceded and concluded the request with the same phrase, 'In this thing the Lord pardon thy servant,' timidly came his problematical plea—'When my master goeth into the house of Rimmon to worship there, and he leaneth on my hand, and I bow myself in the house of Rimmon: when I bow myself in the house of Rimmon,' (yes, this was the rub!), 'the Lord pardon thy servant in this thing.' What would you have answered? What ought a man of God to answer? The scripture has it down in black and white that Elisha said, 'Go in peace', that is to say, he granted the forgiveness he asked, forgiveness for a man who intended to compromise.

2 Complications in modern life

Does this scripture trouble you? Do you wish to explain it away, or rub it out of the Bible altogether? Suppose, however, you are a business man in the modern world, or a politician, or some other kind of public servant, in that case might it not be that you will lay hold of the story of General Naaman with both hands? For it could exactly meet your need and have a word of God for your situation.

When we reach middle life we discover, sometimes to our dismay, that situations exist in which it is impossible to be one hundred per-cent open and stay in public life. No statesman can lay all his cards face up on the table and remain a statesman. And if we assert that all Christians must of necessity all the time lay all cards face up on the table, then we can have no Christian statesmen —to our irreparable loss.

These are the kinds of questions that worry men in business. These are the kinds of questions that make them ask, 'Can a man be a Christian in industry?' Here too is the reason why many public men make only a muted profession of the Christian faith, and why some who are even Church-goers make apologies, 'You know I am not really a religious man' or 'I am only on the way to becoming a Christian'. These apologies are made because these men are essentially good and essentially sensitive. They know from experience that sometimes neither course open is wholly right or wrong, and yet they are forced to choose. Sometimes, indeed, life becomes so tangled that someone is bound to be hurt if a way out for the majority is to be discovered.

When we are young, life presents itself to us in a series of blacks and whites, but as we grow older we begin to wonder if it is possible for even a saint to live untainted in a tainted world. We all partake of the evil around us. Who is there, for example, who has any wish to further slavery, sweated labour, or any other kind of oppression, and yet he may be doing just this by purchasing goods from a country where these things are practised. Can we not now feel a bond between ourselves and this Naaman the Syrian instead of rejecting him as a compromising hypocrite? 'When I go into the supermarket and put my hand into my pocket to purchase an article which I desperately need, but which comes from some communist country or where apartheid is practised, the Lord

pardon thy servant in this thing.'—But will the Lord pardon?
Will my fellow-men pardon?

3 *God's pardon and peace*

We return to the story of General Naaman. There came a day
when after his cure of leprosy by the prophet Elisha in Israel, and
after he had returned home, and presumably worshipped the God
of Israel upon his tiny patch of Israelitish soil, that the King of
Syria declared war against Israel and he was forced to lead the
invading armies, probably by way of the now famous Golan
Heights. Was Naaman so insensitive that he did not agonize over
the terror of his position then as a public servant? This is the
wounding problem for public men, that sometimes because of the
position they hold, they are forced to carry out actions from which
as an individual they would run a mile. Such cases, say hostility to
another country in which they have relatives, or opposition to
some political actions which their friends approve. Church leaders
in two opposing countries sometimes find themselves in situations
of intense awkwardness when those nations go to war. It happened
in 1914 and in 1939. Can we not see how this story of Naaman the
Syrian may have a word from God in all these terrors, even a word
of peace? Public men are not automatically rejected as careless and
callous compromisers.

The blunt fact is that there are situations in life where the good
can only be maintained by compromise. Let the question be put—
would any witness to the real God in Syria have been maintained
had Naaman not transported his two mules' burden of earth and
had he not been willing (at a price), to continue as a public servant
in the Army? Sometimes apparently even God (*mirabile dictu*), is
willing to take what he can get in a confused situation. Please do
not ask for transparent purity in every situation in which God-
fearing men are forced to act. It cannot be, and the Lord will
pardon in the thing if they retain a conscience.

Of course there are dangers. A man, a public servant, may arrive
at the point of deceiving himself. As a direct result of blurring
distinctions he may arrive at the point where he is unable to
distinguish. Spiritual blindness is a possibility for those who make
themselves, or are forced to make themselves walk for a time in the
half light. History warns us of what may be the result if casuistry is
carried too far.

Can we not, however, see a safeguard in Naaman's story, maybe an unsafe safeguard, but a safeguard? Those two mules' burden of earth—they implied on Naaman's part the firm decision to give worship to the true God a regular place in his life.

So this is what we would advise all public men. Give worship a regular place in your private life. You do run grave risks to your personal integrity as public men, but if you expose yourselves to the God who is both righteous and merciful, the God known in Jesus Christ, who became incarnate in a tainted world to save us, you will be in touch with the Saviour of *your* personality in a complicated, tainted world. Hear then the word of God from this story of General Naaman, the word of God for us, 'Go in peace.' God will grant the forgiveness you ask.

23   MEN'S SERVICE

Strength

> 1 Corinthians 16. 13 *'Quit you like men, be strong.'*

What could it be that these Corinthians were about to do that St Paul should appeal to them in such strident terms? 'Quit you like men, be strong.' Were they about to assail in battle the entrenched forces of some opposing army? Was St Paul, like Napoleon at Waterloo committing his élite troops to turn the tide of some desperate conflict? Who were these men to whose basic manhood St Paul was appealing? And what was their situation? And what were they supposed to do?

1 *The setting*

The answer to the first question is that the men were Churchmen, not one hundredth generation Churchmen, nor even second generation Churchmen, but first generation Churchmen, men who had only recently been converted from paganism, men who formed that body of people called the Church in the city where they lived, and men who met from time to time in people's houses for worship. They were a lively, talkative—and if the truth were told—a somewhat showy people, not particularly submissive and certainly not backward in expressing their doubts, dislikes and sharp questionings, even of St Paul.

They lived at Corinth. Corinth was one of the great cities of the

Roman Empire being on the main route from west to east. It was not an old city, this had been completely destroyed by the Romans in 146 B.C. but in the year 46 it had been refounded by Julius Caesar as a Roman 'colony', that is to say, a city founded by the state and inhabited by her citizens. The population, however, quickly became mixed and swelled to more than half a million. Among them would be a large proportion of slaves of Eastern origin and a considerable colony of Jews. Corinth was, in fact, a cosmopolitan city of trade and a city of pleasure. Dominating all was the worship of Aphrodite, the goddess of lust, to whose temple there were attached several hundreds of religious prostitutes. It was also a place of considerable intellectual vitality with prominence given to oratory and argument, though with little purpose beyond argument for argument's sake, so it has left little legacy in this field. Altogether Corinth was flashy, sleazy and vicious.

2 The appeal

What then were those to whom St Paul wrote in those bracing words supposed to do? 'Quit you like men, be strong.' They were being encouraged to stand fast in the faith. Let me quote the whole verse from which my text is a selection, 'Watch ye, stand fast in the faith, quite you like me, be strong.'

Here in the original Greek, in which this letter was written, there are simply four verbs plus the phrase 'in the faith', nothing else. It reads like four strident, staccato siren blasts or four sharp stabs— watch, stand, be manly, be strong.

First, 'watch'. The picture is of a sentry posted high up on the walls of some fortified city—it could be Corinth—scanning the plain on peril of his own life, alert for the slightest indication in the plain that enemy forces might have moved up under cover of darkness waiting to attack. So the Christian must be alert, the tiny Church in Corinth, or London, New York, Paris, Port Durban or Oporto, must be alert or it will be swamped by the secularism, materialism and agnosticism which engulf it. No Christian can afford not to keep himself informed of all that is going on in the world at large and in his own environment. Blame attaches to the sentry, blame attaches to the Christian who is not wide awake to the world the newspapers cover.

Secondly, 'stand'. A sentry asleep on duty in his box commits a punishable offence. It is impossible to sleep standing up. The Christian therefore is bidden to stand. There is to be no armchair

Church, no armchair Christians. We must be ready for action, prepared and equipped to react to whatever the situation suddenly demands.

Thirdly, 'be manly'. This involves standing up, and facing the world like a man. There is to be no sheepish, slouching, soft bearing to our neighbours and contemporaries. 'Let no man despise thee,' wrote Paul to Timothy. 'Let no one despise thy youth.' To stand up and be counted in Corinth as a Christian called for courage of no mean order. To stand for morality in an immoral city, for kindness in a cruel city, for honesty in a corrupt city, meant exposing one's defences to all the enemy's weapons of ridicule, logic and cunning. Unthinkingly people sometimes assume that to be religious is effeminate. To dare to stand fast in the Christian faith, however, calls for a degree of manliness not all are prepared to assert. The need for this manliness is not diminished in the modern western world where the Christian faith is largely discounted as being out of alignment with science. There is great need for Christians 'to gird up the loins of their minds', to resist this defeatism and to attack the false presumptions of science where they are not well-grounded. The need today is for a man's mind and a man's strength.

Fourthly, 'be strong'. The appeal is to that on which men pride themselves, and which women most look for in men—strength. The implication is that men as Christians will be more manly than they would be apart from that profession. They will exhibit the courage to stand alone, to stand against the tide, to stand firm, in place of the drift which is so characteristic of all those who are overcome by mere passing fashions. Jesus was a strong man. This is not appreciated in any superficial estimate of him. The New Testament does, however, record that tough reformer John Baptist as saying, 'After me there comes one stronger than I' and Jesus himself remarked on John Baptist that he was no weak-kneed vacillating character swaying with the breeze like some riverside reed. Everything about the basis of the Christian faith testifies to strength, and the Church at Corinth, and the Church in every age is summoned to a like manly steadfastness.

> 'Soldiers of Christ, arise,
> And put your armour on,
> Strong in the strength which God supplies,
> Through his eternal Son'
>
> (C. Wesley)

3 *The caution*

Perhaps a word of caution is needed. The Christian's strength is not to be a display of wooden obstinacy. The weapons of his warfare are not to be blunt cudgels but swords of finely tempered steel, strength tempered with compassion and deftly wielded, or as the German poet Friedrich von Schiller expresses it, using the metaphor of music instead of combat:

> *Denn wo das Strange mit dem Zarten*
> *Wo starkes sich und Mildes paarten*
> *Da gibt es einen guten Klang*

('Where austerity goes with mildness and strength with gentleness, there is an harmonious sound".)

This is the music of the Christian faith and we are to provide it, stand by it like men in our Corinth, wherever it may be.

24 SPORTSMEN'S SERVICE

Lessons from the arena

1 Corinthians 9. 25 (N.E.B.) '. . . *every athlete goes into strict training.'*

Our Lord Jesus Christ, as far as we know, engaged in no kind of sport, and there are no references to sportsfields, though there is a reference to children playing in the market-place, as Jesus himself must have done as a boy. An absence of references to games is not, however, a charge that can be brought against the New Testament as a whole, St Paul not only lived his life in a civilisation where Olympics were a distinguishing feature, but actually drew some of his most powerful illustrations for his teaching from the world of athletes. We may therefore draw three for ourselves guided by his example. Sport is impossible without rules, it is impossible unless engaged in purposefully, and it is impossible to appreciate it fully without involvement.

1 *Rules*

First, no games can be played without rules. When St Paul wrote to Timothy—(2 Timothy 2. 5), 'no athlete can win a prize unless he has kept the rules', the sight of a Greek arena cannot have been far from his mind's eye. Perhaps he recalled some occasion on which a runner presented himself for the prize and was rejected. Perhaps the runner deliberately crossed in the path of another contestant. Perhaps his qualifications after entry for the race had been discovered as false. Games cannot be played without rules. The question is not whether or not rules are desirable. The fact is that in the nature of the case games are impossible without them. Unless 'the touch line' marks the boundary for all twenty-two players on the football field, as well as for the referee and the linesman, no football can be played.

At the present time we are passing into an age of lawlessness. Everybody wishes to do as he pleases. In the long run, however, lawlessness makes life impossible. Mankind did not take many steps in the direction of civilisation without discovering even at the tribal stage that tribal laws were essential if the tribes were to survive, and without his tribe lonely men could not exist.

Sooner or later every nation, every individual, has to make its choice not whether he will live by any rules at all, but which set of rules will he choose. It is because of this situation that we confidently and unashamedly recommend the discipline of Christ. Yes, it is a discipline, granted it might be summarised as the law of love—'Thou shalt love the Lord thy God with all thy heart, and with all thy soul, and with all thy mind, and with all thy strength . . . and thy neighbour as thyself.' But it is a law. Jesus said, 'On these two commandments hang all the law and the prophets.' There is not a single man who does not know that games require rules. So does life as a whole, and what we plead for is a recognition today of the law of Christ, the law of love between men and God, and men and men.

2 Purposeful living

If one wished to write a comic play, and to do so could be a most salutory occupation, the theme might be adopted of a game of tennis in which no one of the four players strove to win. Imagine each player so polite that he insisted on waving the fact that the second serve really was 'a double fault.' Neither tennis nor any other game can be played without an undeviating purpose.

This again is a theme which St Paul adopted from the arena. 'So run,' he said, 'that you may attain.' The worst attitude in life is to drift. There must always be an aim. Even a sermon needs to have an aim, or it achieves nothing. Without an aim in life, boredom results and boredom could well be described as a psychological wasting disease.

There is an inner connection between faith and purposeful living. In general it is those who do not believe in anything who do not strive for anything. No one needs to be gifted with second sight to observe that in the last decade decaying faith has gone hand in hand with increased boredom. Too many people do not know what they want from life because they do not believe in anything in life, let alone the life hereafter. It is splendid that campaigns should be set on foot to provide more playing fields, for instance, in Britain today. Our modern concrete jungles cry out for more open spaces, but what if people are too bored to exercise their limbs when they have these facilities? It is a sad commentary when schools can no longer get together a first eleven on a Saturday afternoon because it means missing watching some sport on television.

We plead, therefore, for a faith in the hearts and minds of the people in order to combat meaningless and the resulting boredom in the presence of which life folds up. Everyone who plays a game knows he must play to win. Purposefulness is likewise essential for the whole act of living.

3 Involvement

There are two possibilities with regard to games apart from ignoring them altogether, one is to watch them and the other is to play them. That these two approaches are not identical no one will contest. It is true that the critic who sits in the grandstand may see more of the game, but seeing the game is not commitment to the game as is the experience of actually playing it. No one is able to savour the running track unless he has actually run a race on it. He knows nothing of the battle in the mind that has to be won before the battle on the feet. In this twentieth century we have witnessed the virtual apotheosis of the scientific method—but this is to raise a technique too high. The whole truth about life cannot be discovered by the deliberate withdrawal of personal involvement, however legitimate such withdrawal may be for certain limited ends. The existential approach is also necessary, indeed it is to be wondered if the scientist really does avoid it altogether. After all, may he not himself supply the laws of nature which he assumes belong to nature? Is this too philosophical? Then let us return to the practical. To understand what life is about a man must live it. To appreciate what faith is about, a man must exercise it. We plead then, not for grandstand critics of the Christian faith, but for involved performers. 'Run in the race,' says the New Testament. 'Run patiently,' that is, 'like a long distance runner,' and run with an eye on Jesus Christ the file leader and perfector of our faith. This is the way to win in life—to contend in obedience to a discipline, to struggle purposefully and to get down into the arena, into the race itself abjuring the seats of the arm-chair critic.

25   ARTISTS' SERVICE

Matter and Spirit

Genesis 1. 1, 2 (N.E.B.) *'In the beginning of creation, when God made heaven and earth, the heaven was without form and void . . . God said, "Let there be light," and there was light.'*

The designation 'artists' includes all those creative persons who work not only with pigments but also with stone, wood, brick, steel, sounds and even words; that is to say, artists are not only painters but also sculptors, carvers, architects, musicians and writers as well, indeed, all those who try to create something which was not in existence before, using as a tool their own human spirit in order to fashion the medium that is peculiar to them.

There are two obvious elements in the artistic process, the material worked with and the spirit of the artist who works with it. A third element may also be presumed, namely the Universal or Eternal Spirit from whom the inspiration in the artist's creation derives. Moreover, what the artist creates embodies something of that other Spirit which, unlike his own, is Eternal. This is what makes great art live on after the artist is dead, or as William Faulkner described it in his book *Writers at Work*, 'The aim of every artist is to arrest motion which is life, by artificial means, and to hold it fixed so that a hundred years later, when a stranger looks at it, it moves again since it is life.' And also as Nathaniel Hawthorne wrote (*The Marble Faun* 1860) 'Nobody I think ought to read poetry, or look at pictures or statues, who cannot find a great deal more in them than the poet or artist has actually expressed.' What therefore the artist has created is a window on to something eternal because the Eternal Spirit was involved in its creation.

1 *The material*

First, the artist must come to terms with the material with which he works. He cannot by-pass it. What he is trying to express may be pure spirit but it cannot be said without matter. No artist can despise matter. And even if we were given no clear revelation of what is meant by 'the Incarnation' in the Bible we might still have deduced it from the nature of the artists' work. And the reverse is true—the Incarnation of Christ crystalises at one point in history a principle that runs throughout the whole of life.

No, the artist cannot ignore matter, neither can he despise matter, nor treat it lightly. The wood carver must work *with* the grain, the sculptor must know what statues are possible with marble and what with granite, and a great deal else besides as no one even superficially acquainted with Michelangelo's expertise with *pietra serena* will doubt. The painter too must respect the basic laws of colour, and even the writer must understand what words can and cannot do, as the modern study of semantics shows. The artists, we repeat, must treat matter with reverence and it is one of the great merits of the Christian faith that in contradistinction from a number of other great religions this it has consistently done.

2 *The human spirit*

The artist's work, however, is significant because of what it makes with or out of the material it uses. Until it comes into his hands it is raw material. And even life itself, until the artist deploys it, is only raw material. As Paul Klee wrote in *The Inward Vision* (1959) 'Art does not reproduce the visible, rather it makes it visible.' And it does so by manipulation of the material. 'Art,' as Picasso once said, in a daring phrase, 'is a lie that makes us realise the truth', or as Wittgenstein expressed it, perhaps more soberly, 'The work of art is the object seen *sub specie aeternitatis*, in such a way as to have the whole world as a background.'

And none of this can be produced by a Committee but only by an individual. Creativity does not belong to the collective but to the solitary, because it is in the person as person that the spirit resides, and it is from the spirit working with the material that the artist's creation comes. Every artist must therefore be a person.

He must be an individual. He must be allowed to be an individual-ist. Any form of suppression is destructive to all creative artistry. It is in this context that we respect today the protest of Solzhenitsyn.

And every artist's work, be it literature, music, pictures or architecture, must always be to some extent 'a portrait of himself, and the more he tries to conceal himself the more clearly will his character appear in spite of himself.' So wrote Samuel Butler seventy years ago. Indeed, there is some truth in the anonymous saying 'The artist does not see things as they are, but as he is.'

3 The Eternal Spirit

Is it not true, however, that the artist by his work points beyond himself, albeit unwittingly? Does he not in practice preach although he uses no words? Is not the artist a witness to something beyond the surface of things, to an interpretation of the contemporary beyond what the average man grasps? Is he not a seer, proclaiming with pigment, stone, wood or words what he sees? In this sense cannot he be called a prophet, even a preacher? And who will say that his message derives solely from his own spirit? Who will say it is not something which has come to him, in which case he is a revealer of that which belongs to an eternal dimension. Is this too high a plane on which to lift the work of the artist? But suppose it is true (and some of the greatest artists have believed as much) in this case it is right that we should accord the work of artists great honour. In some ways they are the saviours of men.

4 Art and suffering

But artists must pay the price. Creative art is not achieved apart from pain. Perhaps this is nowhere so forcibly expressed in actual artistic work as in the four imprisoned statues by Michelangelo in the Academia in Florence, each figure struggling painfully, as it were, to emerge from the marble, like the story of the creation in the first two verses of the Bible. Creative work labours to bring order out of chaos, light out of darkness, and the process is costly. But if this creative labour is for the welfare of mankind, if it is also redemptive for mankind, and creation and redemption are not separated in the Bible, any more than are the Incarnation and the Cross, we need not be surprised that all great artistic work is costly and every artist has to come to terms with whether or not he is willing to pay the price. Truly *The Agony and the Ecstasy* (1961) was a proper title for Irving Stone's account of the life of Michelangelo. 'Artists must be sacrificed to their art, like the bee, they must put their lives into the sting they give.' So wrote Emerson.

But what of us who do not paint, carve, build or write? We too are artists if we are enriched by their work in our quality of living. The call comes to us to compensate for life's impoverishments by an openness to what the artists have contributed, and art does not only mean an enrichment of culture, it can mean an enrichment of soul, even unto life eternal.

26   ACTORS' SERVICE

Contact with reality

> Colossians 2. 15 (N.E.B.) *'He made a public spectacle of them and led them as captives in his triumphal procession.'*

The world in which St Paul lived was one where the theatre played a prominent rôle. Even today and as long as there is any acquaintance with classical learning, our heritage from the old Greek theatre will be recognized and names like Sophocles and Aristophanes be held in honour. And even though the theatrical art degenerated in the Greek culture with the passage of time, the theatre itself never died away so that the remains of some of the actual theatres in which these plays were performed are visible today being included among the sights on any Hellenic tour. Furthermore, no one can be a master of oratory without becoming aware of Demosthenes and Cicero. All this theatrical background helped to establish the Greek and Roman setting in the cities where St Paul preached. It is not surprising therefore that he should pick on the theatre for one of his most striking illustrations of the cross of Christ. Writing to the Christians at Colossae he said, 'He made a public spectacle of them and led them as captives in his triumphal procession.'

Before we examine this subtle and profound illustration of St Paul to light up the cross of Christ let us review the work of the theatre at a more surface level.

1 Entertainment

The first responsibility of the theatre is to entertain. In some countries as for instance in Italy there is a widespread popular theatre where the day-to-day life of the people is portrayed, often in dialect, with very little other motive than to amuse. Wanda Pasquini plays an important rôle in Florence this way with *La Compagnia del Teatro Populare Toscano.* The value of entertainment must not be underrated for any community. Entertainment breaks up tensions. It is salutory. It may, and sometimes does, lead to salvation, that is, wholeness. For an individual or a community to have nothing else but amusement is bad for both, leading to triviality and superficiality, but to have no amusement at all is to head straight for disaster, psychological and social. Humour (we say) is a saving grace. Even the circus clown has his part to play for the welfare of mankind. To make people laugh can be a god-given ministry.

2 Instruction

The theatre does not, however, only entertain. It instructs. It does this by showing the world its own face. The sight is sometimes frightening, but to exhibit it, nevertheless, is part of its function. At the present time some of the plays on the West End stage really are frightening in the seriousness of their obsession with sex. Bawdiness and vulgarity need not arouse too much anxiety, especially if the result is laughter. The laughter saves. If, however, the modern stage is showing us that the modern world is obsessed with sex seriously, giving its mind and its skill to the exploitation of sex, we need to beware. The theatre instructs, not as in a school room with lesson books, but by holding up a mirror to something in which it cannot help seeing its own clothes, its own preoccupation and its own face, even when they are unacceptable. Nor does the theatre only hold up the surface effects in life for all to see but raises questions concerning the underlying causes. This too is the work of the theatre, if not to provide answers, certainly to raise the significant question. A play succeeds when it has caused the audience to think deeply about life.

3 Dedication

Professional actors are serious people. They have to be. Theirs is a hard life. There are undoubtedly prizes to be won but they come only to the few, and to them not without labour and sacrifice. Every actor has to be dedicated to his art; indeed the care a suc-

cessful stage artist takes over his personal preparation for the part
he has to play could shame some clergymen by comparison. There
are dangers, of course, for actors. They have to play so many parts
in their theatrical career that they may develop into people without
a genuine core to their own personalities. Worship of God can be
the wholesome corrective to this, for in God's presence no part
can be successfully played, only reality counts. In the eternal
presence every one, whatever his calling, must be sincerely what
he is and nothing else, so much so that if the choice had to be made
between cursing God and deceiving God, it would be less danger-
ous to choose the former. This need for a place in his life for
uncompromised reality may have been the reason why the late
Ernest Thesiger, a well-known actor on the London stage for many
years, rarely missed Sunday morning attendance at Church.

4 Christ's theatre

Finally we must turn to a deeper level of thought, represented by
our text. 'He made a public spectacle of them and led them as
captives in his triumphal procession.' The public spectacle was the
crucifixion of Jesus close to a public highway, carried out at a time
when Jerusalem was swollen almost to bursting point with thousands of pilgrims. Pilgrims are always sight-seers. There was no
lack of spectators, no lack of an audience when Christ ascended his
awesome stage called the cross of Calvary.

Let us leave on one side the particular cosmology which was
probably responsible for St Paul's view of Christ's cross as a
triumph over the hostile cosmic powers. Let us concentrate on the
one point that on the cross Christ showed us ourselves as we really
are and it is not a pretty sight. We are men enslaved, enslaved by
passions, prejudices and the sheer weakness of the flesh. The Cross,
like the stage, is a mirror in which the world is able to see its unacceptable face. There we are given a revelation of men's weakness,
but also of God's strength, for in Christ God overcomes the
weakness. So the cross becomes more than a revelation, it becomes
an instrument by which men and women of every age can triumph
over everything that holds them back from achieving the fulness
of their stature. What more fitting then for any actor than to mark
off a place in his life where he worships in the presence of the
crucified, risen Jesus Christ. There is reality, incarnate and eternal,
there is safety for our personality, or in the old language, perhaps
more meaningful, salvation for our souls.

The focal point

> Hebrews 13. 8 (N.E.B.) *'Jesus Christ is the same yesterday, today, and for ever.'*

Exactly one hundred years ago this Church was dedicated, and, shortly after, the first vicar began his ministry in this freshly constituted parish. What a different world it was from what we see around us now! If it were possible by some magic process to be transported back to the parish one hundred years ago we should scarcely know whether to laugh or cry. The buildings would surprise us. The clothes of the people would surprise us—so much black, so many layers and so much thick material. And the pace of life would surprise us—apart from the railway (still something of a wonder), speed was still measured by the ability of the horse.

And suppose, by some magic process, the people of this parish one hundred years ago could be transported, into 1975, they, too, would not know whether to laugh or cry. Imagine a lady aged twenty-five in black bombasine, bonnet and bustle, meeting her counterpart in a mini-skirt or a trouser-suit, or a man in the light-weight clothes of our contemporary style. Imagine the astonishment, even terror of seeing cars hurtling along some motorway, and the noise, the ear-shattering noise, of jet-aircraft making height.

The world, this locality, this parish, have changed almost beyond recognition during the last hundred years, so that we should feel lost if we returned to the old life, and the participants of the old life would feel lost in ours. And yet one feature remains the same, both now and then, so that by it the people both then and now could recognise their whereabouts—that is this Church. It almost alone remains unchanged, proclaiming the faith also unchanged—'Jesus Christ is the same yesterday, today, and for ever.'

As we look back to that world a hundred years ago we are tempted to think of it nostalgically as a time of peace. Actually it was a time of great unease. There was much ignorance, illness and a weaker hold on life. There was more church-going and church building than we see today, but also much hypocrisy, mere conformity and a terrible rift between Church and Chapel. William Gladstone had brought to pass through Parliament many salutary reforms but Disraeli, his successor, said he saw two nations in

Britain and strove to enrich them by building up an empire. France was groaning from the aftermath of the Franco–Prussian war, staggering under the weight of the huge indemnity laid on by the Germans, nursing hopes of revenge; and Germany under William I and Bismark was rebuilding Berlin by leaps and bounds with the money thus obtained, forging the weapons to attack again in less than forty years. France had lost her empire and Germany was building hers without Austria, she suffering from the humiliation of Königsgratz with Franz Josef as the Emperor. Spain was asleep. Italy was taking careful first steps with the experience of a monarchy. Russia under one of the best Tsars that she ever had, Alexander II, keen on reform, was having trouble with the Nihilists who finally took his life.

One hundred years ago, life as now, was full of hopes and fears, of things improved and things got worse, of people loved and people hated, of aims achieved and plans frustrated, of clouds and sunshine, of calm and storm. In a way, it is true, the external aspect of life has completely changed, but substantially it has not changed at all. Pleasure and pain, joy and sorrow, success and failure, health and illness, life and death are still the same as ever they were. They have only altered the colour of their clothes. These basic facts of life are the same, yesterday, today—and we may suppose—for ever.

So let us ask the question. Is the faith the Church proclaims hopelessly outdated? Can we assert that it belongs to the past, only marginally to the present and probably not to the future at all? The answer is, no. We cannot make such statements on any kind of showing. People are the same, life is basically the same and their needs stand out as ever they did.

What are their needs?

1 *A faith*

The people need, as we all need, something in which to believe. After all, what is our basic trouble now? We don't believe in anything. We don't believe in anybody. We are suspicious of top people, suspicious of bottom people. We are suspicious of capital and suspicious of labour. We are suspicious of governments, politicians, business tycoons and news media. Anxiously we wonder, are we being conned, bugged, cheated and misinterpreted? The trouble in Britain today is that we no longer believe, no longer trust. And when a people no longer believes in anything the quality of its life drops down, even its money is of lesser value.

2 A foothold

What do the people, what do we all need today? A firm basis for living. We need a foothold across the shifting swamps of life on to which to plant our feet. We have come to a point in history now where we almost make a change for the change's sake. And the result, the all-but-shattering result, is not refreshment but a wearisome sameness. Go where you will in the world, to Wednesbury, Wyoming, Westminster or Wigan, always the change is to the 'high-rise block', to identical skylines, the unending concrete and the myriads of square little windows. But changing cities, changing fashions, changing modes of shopping even, can only grant us satisfaction if under our feet is a firm foundation. Where do we come from? Why are we here? And what is our destiny? Without answers to these basic questions, be they at best faith answers, all our changes bring us discontent. People today need a basis for living as they did a hundred years ago. We have not really changed.

3 Individual worth

What do we need? We need a new belief in the worth of every individual. Mechanisation and industrialisation were coming on apace in Britain one hundred years ago. Men and women who were craftsmen in the social community became mere 'hands' in the factories that rattled and whined. So there rose up rows and rows of little standard houses and rows and rows of little standard people with mass production levelling them even more in a monotony of repetitive labour. And let us not imagine that all of this is now behind us. Today there is a more subtle, sinister style of conditioning of individuals, turning them into tools of other people, whereby by means of the box in the corner, the television screen, thinking the thoughts we all must think, selecting the clothes we all must wear, and even the processed foods that we shall eat tomorrow. So the electronic age is reducing men and women to a few holes punched in some computor card, so individuals are being ironed out to be alike, and the unrest of our time may be in fact the protest.

Here then this Church stands, and many others like it, to minister to the needs of men and women, providing something, proclaiming some one in whom we can believe, a foundation for our feet to stand upon in a time of overwhelming change and a value placed upon the worth of every individual of whatever colour, class or creed. The Church proclaims there is Jesus Christ still to believe in, there is the faith 'once delivered to all the saints' on which you can safely plant your feet, offering you forgiveness, new life, joy and a hope beyond the grave, and not only that, but the love of God caring for you as an individual different from your neighbour, important each for yourselves alone.

What should be the keynote of this Church centenary? Surely thanksgiving, eucharist, the word eucharist means thanksgiving. 'Lift up your hearts.' 'We lift them up unto the Lord.' What for? For those benefactors who gave this building and endowed it. For that line of clergy who have ministered in and from these walls. Thanksgiving for the Bishop who oversees the work, but above all for 'Jesus Christ, the same yesterday, today, and for ever,' by means of whose life, death and resurrection we are gathered here. Everything derives from Jesus Christ. Everything is owed to Jesus Christ. To be a Christian is first and last to look to him. Let that be our focal point at this hundredth anniversary, for when this is the case the Church is very strong, indeed, the gates of hell cannot prevail against it.

28 DEANERY SYNOD DEDICATION SERVICE

Today we begin a new three year term in the history of our Deanery Synod and those of us gathered here are responsible for carrying it. What are we supposed to be doing? Let us face it, we are charged with the responsibility of helping to administer organized religion in this geographical area called our Deanery.

In a way this hurts. It hurts because anyone with only half an eye can see that both organized religion and administration are out of fashion. The signs of the times are very different—the rise of the problematical Jesus movement, the gathering momentum of the Pentecostal approach in all the Churches, and the growing interest in prayer and meditation at least on the part of the young. Not one of these indications of the contemporary weathervane points to any blowing of the wind of the Spirit in the direction of organized religion and of administration. That is why I say that in a way time given to membership of a Deanery Synod hurts. We wonder if it is time wasted.

1 *The Church is a household*

It is well, however, to remember that the Church of God is the household of God. In a household there are the festive occasions, the social occasions, the outgoing activities and a whole way of life; but some one has to decide on the amount of the insurance premium, some one has to order the groceries, some one has to be in touch with the doctor, the dentist, the Town Hall and many other organizations besides, if that household is to function and remain safe. No household can be run if the chores are dodged.

Surely there can be no doubt that the prime tasks of the Church are evangelistic outreach and worship. But there can also be no doubt that the task will fail unless our administration is sound. That is why time given to the Deanery Synod is not wasted. It is making safe the household of God for outgoing activity.

2 *Searching questions*

But are we concerned with outgoing activity in our Deanery? Have we been concerned with it in these last three years of our Synod's history? Have we fallen victims to the temptation that because our administration has been smooth, efficient and orderly, we have more than justified our existence? How much has the evangelistic outreach of the Church here been forwarded by our Synodical administration?

These are searching questions and we could be confused by them. We could be confused into despising the Synod and that would be wrong. We could be confused into imagining that the Synod has to become an evangelising agency and that too would be wrong. The Synod is not a Church. It is a committee, but its sights should constantly be lifted from itself to ask how far it is helping the Churches in its area to fulfil the special task each one is called to undertake.

In some areas the functions of each Church differ greatly from each other. In a sense, however, each Church is not justifying itself if it is like the Church next door but only if it is unlike it. All the same, each Church must accept the Church next door, and it is surely one of the chief functions of this Synod to hold the differing

Churches in a bond of unity together. It is even true that failure to assume responsible membership of the Synod constitutes a failure to recognise and foster the one aim of the household of God in this district.

To come down to earth, it may not be possible for Churches in some localities to unite in any one particular activity, the differences may be too great, not least by reason of the area they have to serve. But Churches could take far more interest in each other than they do. They could pray more for each other and they could support more than they do any one Church when it makes a particular effort or undertakes some particular enterprise.

3 Practical advice

As then we set out on another three year chapter of the Synod's history, let us be open-eyed in accepting ourselves for what we are—a body of people charged with administration of the household of God, a household which must have administration if it is to function adequately.

Secondly, let us see to it that we know why we are giving our time to administration. It is in order that the gospel of Christ may be made even more available than it is both by word and by sacrament, and by practical action in secular fields.

And thirdly, let us never be weary in the well-doing of keeping the Churches together, bearing one another's burdens, encouraging one another amid the difficulties of our common task and seeing the Synod as an instrument of a unity of Spirit.

In which thing if we do not fail, we shall more than justify our existence, and time given to our meetings need not hurt. We shall have played a necessary part in the ordering of the household of God and earn that commendation which the Lord made in his parable of the servants of the household 'Well done, thou good and faithful servant. Thou hast been faithful over a few things, I will make thee ruler over many things: enter thou into the joy of thy Lord.' Matthew 25. 23.

Being, doing, speaking

> Job 2. 13 *'For seven days and seven nights they sat beside him on the ground, and none of them said a word to him; for they saw that his suffering was very great.'*

The other day a friend of mine told me an experience of his. 'I began,' he said, 'the parochial part of my ministry a month before the outbreak of war in 1939. I express it so because I had already been ordained two years but had spent the time as a theological college tutor. I knew little about parish work and learned even less from my Rector because in those days clergy did not retire at seventy and this one was well past that milestone. So I had to learn the hard way. My wife and I lived in a house adjoining a hospital, that is to say, there was only a party wall between us, and one of my self-imposed tasks was to visit there. One occasion I remember to this day. The war was well under way and the town was filled with troops. One night, long after we had gone to bed, there was an insistent rapping on our wall on the hospital side. I pulled on some clothes and ran round to enquire the reason, only to be greeted by the Matron with the news that a young woman was dying. I had never seen death before and had no idea what to do. But it was too late to do anything anyway. I saw what I presumed was her last breath and watched the transformation take place which even those accustomed to it find awesome. But the scene was disturbed by a young airman I had scarcely noticed crouching by her bed. Suddenly he broke down. I had never seen a man cry before, certainly not a man in uniform and certainly not cry like that. But instinct somehow made me turn to him, put my arm round his shoulder and lead him out to another room. And there I sat (I cannot tell you how long), my arms round the stranger, saying nothing because 'I saw that his suffering was very great.' The young woman was his wife and it was a case of puerperal fever after the birth of their first child.

1 *Silence*

Now let us return to the book of Job and to the text. It is possible that we do not hold Eliphaz, Bildad and Zophar in high regard. Eliphaz was pompous, Bildad was dried up with orthodoxy, and Zophar thought he knew all the answers. Nevertheless, these three friends of Job were sensitive and men can be forgiven much if they are sensitive. When these three heard of Job's plight they left their homes to comfort him, and when they saw him, scarcely able to believe their eyes at the sorry state to which illness had reduced him, 'for seven days and seven nights' (oh yes, we can read this as poetic exaggeration), 'they sat beside him on the ground, and none of them said a word to him; for they saw that his suffering was very great.'

There are times when the proper ministry is to say nothing. When people are in desperate trouble, if preachers have any instinct at all, if any sensitivity, the proper course is to say nothing. Eliphaz, Bildad and Zophar had something to their credit because when they saw their friend 'none of them said a word to him; for they saw that his suffering was very great.'

Could it be that the suffering of the world at this time is so very great that the proper ministry for the Church now is to say nothing, to give up preaching and to spend its whole strength instead in putting its arms around suffering humanity? There are times when words are out of place. No one chatters when a woman is struggling to give birth to a child; no one opens his mouth when it is obvious that the man in the bed over there is near the end of his road; and when love really hits you, it all but silences you, for in that hour words sound trite and futile. 'There is a time to speak and a time to refrain from speaking,' says the book of Proverbs and I shall not blame the man who feels that that time is now, it will at least show that he is sensitive, a first requisite in my judgement for a Christian pastoral ministry.

2 Empty preaching

But Eliphaz, Bildad and Zophar in the book of Job only remained silent for seven days and seven nights, thereafter they talked 'nineteen to the dozen.' The book is all but filled with their words and how boring they are, superficial and defensive. What happened? You can read for yourself what happened. Job began to talk. In a way it was terrible talk, almost godless talk, the talk of a man whose bodily pain drives him to hit out, after which what Eliphaz, Bildad and Zophar did, each in turn, each worse than the other, was to talk to his talk, to argue to his arguments, to try to knock him down where he was knocking down—in other words they preached at him, which is a travesty of preaching. It is a ministry of empty words.

Peace came to Job apart from his comforters. This is the galling part of this story, but peace of mind comes to a man when he experiences the real presence of God however the consciousness of that presence may be mediated. It may be through some event in the natural order (there are examples of that in scripture), it may be through some beneficial action, it may be through words spoken; but they will never be mere words, never empty words.

When in our worship we pass from the ministry of the word to the ministry of the sacrament, as I understand it, we pass to the sacrament of the real presence of God, but more striking still the real presence of God broken. 'This is my body,' says the priest as he breaks the bread. 'This is my blood' as he pours the wine. The broken presence of God, the presence of the broken God (a thought startling enough to make the mind reel), this is what ministers to us in our brokenness, and preaching which ministers this is never empty. Eliphaz, Bildad and Zophar were never so close to ministering the God they ineptly failed to convey by their speeches as when they sat silently with Job, hurt by the hurt they witnessed in him. This is how they should have spoken if they were to speak at all.

3 *Preaching from sensitive experience*

And yet preaching there must be, a 'ministry of the word' there must be. Everywhere the Bible testifies to its use as an instrument. The spoken word, by the Spirit, can become an instrument of the real presence of God, the broken God, as can the sacrament. We must see preaching as an effective instrument; but it never will be an effective instrument as long as it is counted as mere rhetoric, oratory or elocution (*la langue bien pendue*, 'the tongue well hung'). The ministry of the word that moves men and moves situations is the word that comes out of silence, the silence of the speaker confronted with his own pain, his friend's pain, his enemies' pain, and their joys, the word that comes from the preacher when he puts his arms round the broken man and dare not trust himself to speak for he feels too broken himself; but the preacher who in that silence, that brokenness or that exhilaration has also encountered the real presence of God . . . when that man speaks people listen because God is there and they are healed; not because of the oratory or even the theology, which may be thin, but because the word has become flesh and tabernacled among us. If that is not so, how shall we understand the chequered history of preaching?

Application

So let us frame our priorities aright. The first necessity for us all is to be, and by the time a man is fifty he is even responsible for his own face.

Secondly, we have to do, not forgetting how our Lord warned against using good works as a publicity device. 'Do gooders' can be hypocritical.

Thirdly, we have to speak, speak to man's condition, not to his arguments, and this means coming close to people, understanding people because we have faced up to ourselves in the silence of God's presence.

The Christian ministry questioned, underrated and despised, as it may be, offers the finest opportunity to live out these priorities, and where they are lived out, there will be encountered the finest preaching, a ministry of the Word, that is an *Ereigniss prache* as the Germans express it—a speaking event, an event in which God works by his Spirit, an event which can even be a new creation, or as the first chapter of Genesis expresses it—'And God said, "let there be". . . . and there was.'

30   CLERGY RETREAT

Our limited ministries

Matthew 15. 24 (N.E.B.) *'I was sent to the lost sheep of the house of Israel, and to them alone.'*

In its context this statement rings a harsh note and you cannot soften it by the way you speak it. Picture the scene. A woman crouching at our Lord's feet convulsed with sobs, telling through her tears in Canaanitish dialect of her daughter's lunacy. A mother's love for a child who is an idiot one may find stupefying at first but one soon learns to appreciate it and to understand that this woman might well tramp the countryside to crave her daughter's healing from the man who could hold that possibility; but when she encountered him, she encountered refusal. 'I was sent to the lost sheep of the house of Israel, and to them alone.' His ministry did not extend beyond the territorial boundaries of Israel. His calling was in fact parochial.

What would you have done in this situation? Surely there is not a priest with a ministry as long as mine, or not as long, who has not faced this situation of a woman weeping? What would you do? Some priests are harsh. I have heard of more than one, sought out by a woman with a broken marriage, who have shut the Vicarage door—'I can do nothing for you. You have come to the wrong address.'

1 Compassion which strengthens

First, this story, for all its apparent harshness, reminds us of the nature of Christ's compassion. It is always strong, far-seeing and unsentimental.

Did you ever see a play by Frederic Knott called *Wait until Dark?* It was a thriller set in the basement of a seedy house in Notting Hill Gate in which Honor Blackman played the part of a young housewife, blinded by a car accident. Blind, however, though she was, she nevertheless foiled three thugs who entered her apartment, reacting with a fine feminine courage. How had she acquired such courage? Largely through her husband's strong, far-seeing, unsentimental compassion. You watch him with her for a few minutes at the opening of the play, wondering at his tactics. Awkwardly in her new experience of a sightless world, she had dropped something. But her husband did not retrieve it although she asked for it. Pathetically she groped for it across the carpet. 'Warmer! Warmer!' he teased. 'Now try twelve o'clock.' It seemed cruel. But by this treatment she recovered the object herself, after which he presented her with six spanking kisses in consolation. That was sympathy of the strong variety, the sympathy which imparts strength, making for independence, utterly unlike the soft sympathy which weakens, degrades and is all but useless in its outcome.

Is not this a window on the compassion of Christ? Yes, his refusal of the plea of this Canaanitish woman reads harshly, but that she persisted with her request suggests that she heard some deeper note below the refusal, indeed, he gave the good news she could scarcely believe; but not until he had evoked a faith in himself, sturdy and independent. Jesus did not merely express sympathy. It does not appear from the gospel records that he ever murmured 'I am sorry for you.' Always his compassion issued in action, always it was aimed at encouraging the growth of independent strength; for without this issue, compassion can be a debilitating exercise.

2 *Informed by principle*

And now we turn to our ministries. They should be informed by principle. Nothing is easier in the life of a priest than that his days should be actuated by drift. Our time is our own. Episcope does not extend to watching how long we spend in the armchair. Unlike factory workers we do not 'clock in.' Some priests do little hard work. Some priests work exceedingly hard. A great many, observing the futility of both extremes, aim merely at appearing kind. All three groups fail in final achievement because their lives are lacking in principle. This is what we see in Jesus—a ministry informed by principle. 'I was sent to the lost sheep of the house of Israel, and to them alone.'

May I draw your attention to the actions Jesus did not pursue? The 'rich young ruler' advised to keep the commandments was left to go his own way, still deficient in the one thing needful. The nine cleansed lepers who did not even return to our Lord to say 'thank you' were not pursued with a lesson on gratitude. The unrepentant dying malefactor crucified with Jesus was not worked upon by the Saviour to make him change his mind, which is more *laissez-faire* than most evangelists would tolerate. Our Lord did not leave the early Church any impression of being hectically busy or impatiently urgent in his ministry. He did not appear to worry over innocent suffering as we worry. Certainly he faced this sobbing Canaanitish woman with her idiot daughter tormenting her mind, able even in that moving moment to adhere to a ministry motivated by principle. 'I was sent to the lost sheep of the house of Israel, and to them alone.' Or as the writer of the fourth gospel comments on another scene—'He himself knew what he would do.'

Every now and again, and especially perhaps on a Retreat, we come face to face with the problem how we are to squeeze from life the time to fulfil all the works expected of us. For the most part a priest's life is occupied not with great tasks but with a great number of little tasks. How can he manage? By learning from our Lord that to attempt everything is to act in default of principle. We must accept the idea of limitation in our ministry. To do everything is impossible. There is a Chinese proverb which says, 'A bird can roost but on one branch. A mouse can drink no more than its fill from a river,' but John Locke's comment is even more penetrating in his *Essay Concerning the Human Understanding*. 'It is of great use to the sailor to know the length of his line, though he cannot with it fathom all the depths of the ocean.'

The great necessity for all priests is to exercise a ministry informed by the principle that his ministry must be a limited one, as Jesus' was—'I was sent to the lost sheep of the house of Israel and to them alone.'

3 The parish priest

Now we turn to apply the text more closely. It is remarkable that Christ, the *Salvator Mundi*, should be 'sent to the lost sheep of the house of Israel, and to them alone.' Surely a statesmanlike assessment would have required that the Incarnation took place in Rome and not Bethlehem, Judaea was a troublesome backwater and Galilee provincial. I observe, however, that when our Lord despatched his apostles during his lifetime on earth on a mission-tour, his restriction was imposed on them. 'Do not take the road to the Gentile lands and do not enter any Samaritan town; but go rather to the lost sheep of the house of Israel.' Apparently with the commission there went the limitation. If so with the Lord, if so with the apostles, can I count myself the exception? Must not every priest accept a limited ministry? And if in protest we cry out that Paul tramped the Roman roads of the Gentile lands, I shall have to remind you and myself (for sometimes I also cry out), that for much of the time Paul was chained to a guard and could not tramp at all, and when he did there was always the 'thorn in the flesh' holding him back.

Not long ago I received a letter from an accomplished parish priest who complained bitterly how our calling today is a marginal one. We are not required to be welfare officers any more, or educationalists, or social planners. We suffer banishment to the Vestry and are dubbed 'Establishment men.' The world stands us in the margin of its modern life as traditional and irrelevant.

There is truth in this diagnosis. In most front line areas, and television has made almost the whole country come into this category, the parson has no accepted status. Oh yes, we are trusted a bit more because of our collars, but by and large we have no status except to identify with the television programme *All Gas and Gaiters*. So the parish priest has nothing but himself, his faith, his ability and also, I suppose, his face. Then let us start there on the scratch line and even thank God for this limitation. Jesus saved the world from the limitation of a ministry confined to 'the lost sheep of the house of Israel,' living as a Jew with restrictions which only a reading of the Pentateuch can help us to grasp. Yet men crowded round him because he was a man, self-authenticating, a man who lived by faith and principle.

I have a restricted life. There are many things I would like to do in my ministry but they are just not possible. Any priest who has tried to work in a city centre will understand. I have known restriction since I was ordained. So have you, I guess. Apparently it is to limited ministries that God has sent us. There will be no peace, no strength and no succour available for others till we live by this principle. Of course the grass is greener, or so we imagine, on the other side in my neighbour's parish. And how well I could have done in my ministry had I 'a blue' a 'triple first', or even a golden voice. And as for these parishioners . . . do you know they even like Mattins! How much better I could have done if only. . . . Do you know the poems of that Welsh clergyman R. S. Thomas? You should read them. 'God! Is this the plot I have been given? All these rocks? Then I must make a rock-garden!' I don't wonder Jesus was strong. I don't wonder his compassion was strong. I don't wonder he could deal strongly with this Canaanitish woman weeping over her idiot child. He had accepted a ministry with limitations which sets a man's life in the mould of principle and makes him a comforter, a strengthener. It is what I should like to be by God's good grace in my restricted calling.